The Economic Future of American Families

**FRANK S. LEVY AND
RICHARD C. MICHEL**

The Economic Future of American Families

Income and Wealth Trends

THE URBAN INSTITUTE PRESS
Washington, D.C.

THE URBAN INSTITUTE PRESS
2100 M Street, N.W.
Washington, D.C. 20037

Library of Congress Cataloging in Publication Data

Levy, Frank, 1941—
The economic future of American families: income and wealth trends/ Frank S. Levy and Richard C. Michel.

Includes bibliographical references.

1. Income distribution—United States   2.   Wealth—United States.   3.   Family—United States.   I.   Michel, Richard C.   II.   Title.

HC110.I5L472   1991   90-20278
339.2′0973--dc20   CIP

ISBN 0-87766-487-0 (alk. paper)
ISBN 0-87766-486-2 (alk. paper; casebound)

Urban Institute books are printed on acid-free paper whenever possible.

Printed in the United States of America.

Distributed by:
            University Press of America
4720 Boston Way   3 Henrietta Street
Lanham, MD 20706   London   WC2E 8LU   ENGLAND

THE URBAN INSTITUTE is a nonprofit policy research and educational organization established in Washington, D.C., in 1968. Its staff investigates the social and economic problems confronting the nation and government policies and programs designed to alleviate such problems. The Institute disseminates significant findings of its research through the publications program of its Press. The Institute has two goals for work in each of its research areas: to help shape thinking about societal problems and efforts to solve them, and to improve government decisions and performance by providing better information and analytic tools.

Through work that ranges from broad conceptual studies to administrative and technical assistance, Institute researchers contribute to the stock of knowledge available to public officials and private individuals and groups concerned with formulating and implementing more efficient and effective government policy.

Conclusions or opinions expressed in Institute publications are those of the authors and do not necessarily reflect the views of other staff members, officers, or trustees of the Institute, advisory groups, or any organizations that provide financial support to the Institute.

ACKNOWLEDGMENTS

The authors have a great many people to thank for their contributions to the research for this book. At The Urban Institute, Brenda Brown, Patrick Purcell, Kyna Rubin, and Felicity Skidmore all contributed in various ways to the quality of both the analysis and the writing in the volume. Some of this work was also done while one of the authors (Levy) was in residence at The Brookings Institution. At Brookings, Chuck Byce, Chrissy de Fontenay, Caroline Ratcliffe, Amy Salsbury, and Lorelei Stewart were all instrumental in producing the data that underpin many of our arguments.

Thanks also go to Edward Wolff of New York University and an anonymous referee for insightful comments on an early draft of this book. Dr. Wolff deserves special credit for suggesting changes that corrected a number of anomalies in the wealth data that we could not initially explain.

Above all, we would like to thank The Ford Foundation's Urban Poverty Program for its generous financial support to The Urban Institute to complete this project. In particular, our two project officers, Gordon Berlin and Robert Curvin, were very supportive and patient in waiting for us to sort through our data before finally reaching some conclusions.

Any errors, judgments, or omissions are, of course, the sole responsibility of the authors and do not necessarily reflect the views of The Urban Institute or The Ford Foundation.

Frank S. Levy
Richard C. Michel

CONTENTS

Tables

Figures

FOREWORD

The Urban Institute's interest in tracking, projecting, and understanding changes in the economic status of Americans dates back to the origins of the Institute more than two decades ago. It was clear then as it is today that few major public policies can be fully or fairly appraised without understanding their implications for the distribution of income.

A combination of slow growth in earnings and income since the 1970s and an increase in the number of children being raised in single-parent homes has increased the inequality of income distribution across American families. The most disturbing aspect of this growing gap is that it reflects and, in turn, affects the unequal distribution of opportunity in society. Children of people in the low end of the income distribution do not have the same opportunities as those in the high-income categories. This fact undermines the promise that most Americans believe our country symbolizes.

This book documents the effects of the past, present, and future economy on different generations, genders, and races. Some of the authors' findings—that both white and black young families are faring worse than their parents' generation in some important respects, that the less educated are at an acute economic disadvantage compared to their more educated peers, and that the economic status of young black families has declined relative to that of young white families—may not make front page news. Why is this?

We have learned to live too easily with the fact of economic inequality in this country. First, we allow ourselves to be distracted by current crises without giving sustained attention to long-term social problems. Second, we are doubtful, as a nation, that there can be public solutions to what we perceive to be private problems, i.e., that government institutions can make lasting improvements in personal or family lives. Last, many people feel it is up to individual families to solve their own problems, which has promoted independence but has also fostered insensitivity to the plight of those left behind. Because of this public attitude, leaders deal with these problems only episodically or partially, and many lack the breadth of vision and foresight to see that these growing gaps are serious and have the potential to impair the economic futures of all of us.

This book, like a growing proportion of Institute research, cuts across specific programs and populations to examine broad national economic issues. The importance of the authors' findings underscores the need for private foundations and the federal government to support broad studies of this nature, the implications of which should concern all Americans.

William Gorham
President

Chapter One

INTRODUCTION AND OVERVIEW

In recent years, U.S. public opinion polls have reported a mixed economic message: people are generally satisfied with the present economy but worried about the future.[1] Fear of the future based on uncertainty about what other countries may do to us or a sense that we have arrived on "the downside of history" often reflects external forces. But fear for the future also stems from an unarticulated concern about the long-run impacts of our current social and economic behavior.

One central issue is our willingness to provide for the future. The economic prospects of the United States depend upon our level of capital accumulation and the quality of our future workforce. These, in turn, depend upon decisions we make today: the rate at which we save, the rate at which we make physical investments, and the way in which we raise and educate the current generation of children.

Unfortunately, how well our future is provided for does not depend entirely on our decisions as individuals. A single individual can save at a high rate, but his long-term standard of living will depend on his income, which, in turn, is tied to the productivity and capital stock of the whole economy. A parent who educates his child well ensures the child will do well relative to other children, but the child's absolute standard of living will be affected by average living standards in the economy, which, in turn, are related to the quality of the entire workforce.[2] In economic terms, this is the collective goods problem.

Collective goods embody a temptation to cheat. Most goods benefit only those who pay for them. The benefits of collective goods by their nature cannot be so restricted. Security protection is an easy example. If my neighbor pays for a security guard to watch his property, I also benefit. But if I do not share the cost he may drop his protection and I will lose as well. Savings and education decisions share the same property. But the temptation to cheat is made worse when the benefits of cheating (more consumption) occur today while the costs occur in the future.

If I save less, I can increase my current consumption. As long as everybody else continues to save at high rates, the effect of my decreased saving on the nation's future capital stock will be infinitesimal. And while I feel the responsibility to educate my own children, I may not want to pay additional taxes to educate other people's children, in the hope that the quality of the workforce will somehow take care of itself.[3]

A low rate of capital accumulation does not necessarily result in an immediate economic collapse that might draw public attention. Instead, it leads to a slow grinding down of growth, and the economic mobility carried with it, that occurs over decades. A failure to adequately educate today's children leads to a similar slow decline. Thus, it becomes clear that focusing national attention on underinvestment (human or physical) is far more difficult than focusing national attention on, say, inflation—a different collective problem that has immediate impacts and whose costs can be seen in every trip to the supermarket.[4]

Over the last decade, evidence has grown that U.S. provisions for the future are weak. Beginning in 1982, the federal government began to run large budget deficits, which grew in size despite the economic recovery that followed. Also in 1982, the personal savings rate began to fall from 7 percent of disposable personal income (an average it had maintained through the 1970s) to the 3 to 4 percent range of 1985–1987. Lower personal savings combined with federal government *dissavings* caused the national savings rate (households, businesses, and government combined) to fall from 16.9 percent of GNP in 1971–1973 to 12.8 percent of GNP in 1985–1987. The nation's rate of investment also declined from 16.7 percent of GNP in 1971–1973 to 15.8 percent in 1985–1987. The decline in investment was more gradual than the decline in national savings only because a growing proportion of U.S. investment is now financed from foreign countries—one result of a large trade deficit, which suddenly grew in the early to mid 1980s.[5]

Changes in the economic condition of children to some extent paralleled changes in the rate of savings. Between 1973 and 1986, the number of children in families with incomes below $10,000 (in 1987 dollars) rose from 7.5 million to 10.1 million. Because these were years of low birth rates, a growing *number* of low-income children meant a sharp increase in the *proportion* of children in families with incomes under $10,000, (a proportion that went from 10 percent in 1973 to 16 percent in 1986. Part of this increase reflected the growing number (and proportion) of children in female-headed families. But the increase also reflected the effects of a generally stagnant economy and a number of two-parent families that lost income in the 1980–1982 recession and did not subsequently recover. While the proportion of children in female-headed families increased, so did the proportion of children in two-earner families, leading to a growing inequality in children's circumstances.[6]

This book seeks to understand the future consequences of current trends. Many observers speculate that today's young workers will not live as well as their parents did.[7] Although we cannot know the future with certainty, we can do the calculations to see whether this outcome is actually implied by current slow growth rates. Similarly, discussions of the low personal savings rate suggest that today's young families will be unprepared for retirement. Is this true? Do current savings rates mean that young families will accumulate less wealth (vis-à-vis their income) than earlier generations did?

In examining these questions, we have tried, where possible, to look both at the population as a whole and at groups within the population—that is, persons classified by age, education, and so on. Disaggregated analysis is important because, for example, young high-school-educated and college-educated workers have had sharply different experiences in recent years.

One can object that this kind of study is distracting. If our estimates suggest anything less than Armageddon, which they do, people can say: "See, when you look at the future, it does not look so bad after all despite our current problems." We disagree. Some of the current discussions of undersaving are couched in easily dismissed bombastic rhetoric. Our purpose is to replace rhetoric with numbers that describe future U.S. economic life based on current trends. Our hope is that concrete numbers make it harder to avoid considering the consequences of an unwillingness to provide for the future.

The body of our research is presented in seven chapters. Chapter 2 examines trends in individual income growth in the post-World War II period and shows how the nation moved from rapid income growth (1946–1973) to slower growth bordering on stagnation (1973–1986). Although slow income growth has only recently become an issue, we show how it contributes to a context in which many issues, such as fear of a vanishing middle class and the growth of the federal budget deficit, fit together.

Chapter 3 looks at post-1973 incomes in greater detail and shows that while average incomes were generally stagnant, women, especially women with college educations, earned moderately higher incomes than the average, while young men who had not gone beyond high school earned much less than the average. We show how the declining demand for manufacturing employment helps explain the decline in income for high-school-educated young men.

In chapter 4 we turn from individual incomes to family incomes and family income distribution. The economic trends between 1973 and 1986 created a family income distribution with moderately more inequality and, equally important, with significant shifts of the kinds of families at the bottom of the income distribution. Elderly families moved from the bottom of the distribution to the lower middle, while their vacated places at the bottom were taken by the growing number of female-headed families. Because of these movements, income inequality among families with children has increased far more rapidly than income inequality among all families.[8] In particular, the combination of greater inequality and income stagnation means that the proportion of children in families with incomes below $10,000 has risen from one in ten (in 1973) to one in six today.

In chapter 5 we parallel our discussion of family income with an examination of trends in family asset accumulation. Our findings show that, like family income and wage growth, the growth in per household assets or wealth was considerably lower in the 1970s than in the 1950s. This wealth slowdown began much earlier than the income stagnation, however. Older families, that is, members of the generation of baby boomer parents, appear to have been unaffected by the wealth slowdown, and as a result they were able to achieve remarkable gains in wealth.

On average, members of the baby boom generation experienced positive growth in their net wealth, though this growth was not nearly as high as that of preceding generations. As is the case with income, less educated young persons in the 1980s seem to face a more uncertain prospect for net wealth growth than more educated young persons.

The last three chapters of the book turn to the future. In chapter 6 we project the future path of wages and family incomes for young workers. These projections ultimately depend on the growth of productivity in the economy, something we cannot predict with accuracy, so we construct wage and income growth trends under two alternative scenarios: one reflecting a continuation of recent productivity growth, the other reflecting a consensus estimate of optimistic productivity growth, with separate projections for high-school and college-educated workers. In chapter 7 we extend our analysis of income growth to examine future trends in the accumulation of assets, and in chapter 8 we summarize our research and offer recommendations on potential policy solutions to the problems we have identified.

Notes

1. See, for example, the poll in *U.S.A. Today*, January 25, 1988, pp. 1–2.

2. The prospect of earning a *relatively* high wage but in a poor economy is one of the factors behind the "brain drain" that affects many low-income countries.

3. Even in this regard, the past decade has seen a decreasing proportion of college costs born by parents and an increasing proportion born by the students themselves. See Astin et al. (1989).

4. Put differently, the economic problem facing President Bush—undersaving—is more difficult to attack politically than the inflation that faced President Reagan.

5. For a good discussion of the "twin deficits" and the relationship between them, see Isabel Sawhill 1988, Stone 1988, and Lawrence 1988. For a more technical analysis of the same, see Helliwell 1990.

6. During the 1973–1986 period, the proportion of children in two-*parent* families declined. But among two-parent families, the increase in mothers' labor force participation increased so fast that the proportion of children in two-*earner* families actually rose.

7. For example, see Moynihan 1987.

8. This is because the growing number of female-headed families at the bottom of the income distribution was offset in statistics for all families by the rising incomes of the elderly, as described in more detail in chapter 4.

Chapter Two

SETTING THE CONTEXT: THIRTEEN YEARS OF STAGNANT WAGES

A central fact of our book is the way in which the years since World War II divide into two major periods: 27 years of rapid real wage growth followed by at least 13 years of real wage stagnation.[1] In a world of inflation, unemployment, and budget and trade deficits, the rate of real wage growth may not seem like the best single indicator of economic performance. But we shall show that once one understands the role of wage growth in economic life, many other economic issues—the question of vanishing middle class jobs, the federal budget deficit, the trade deficit—begin to fall into place.

We sometimes picture a career as a process of pushing up a crowded flight of stairs, elbowing past competitors along the way.[2] This picture implies that the pay raises we get reflect merit alone. The truth is more complex. Our merit determines our advancement vis-à-vis other workers, but the purchasing power in any pay increase reflects both our merit and the economic health of the economy (and of our employer). In a healthy economy, rising labor productivity—i.e. rising output per worker—creates a substantial amount of extra purchasing power for raises and so most workers can see their paychecks grow in absolute terms. The pushing and shoving is still there but it takes place on an up-escalator rather than a flight of stairs: some people gain ground faster than others, but most people make progress as the whole wage scale rises.

We can see this rising wage scale by following an income benchmark over time—for example, the median annual income of 45- to 54-year-old men who worked year round and full time (table 2.1). The income figures throughout this book are before taxes. By 1986, the oldest baby-boomers (born in the late 1940s) had not yet turned 45, so incomes of men in this age range were not yet affected by big changes in cohort size. By focusing on men who work year round and full time, we can isolate the effects of rising real wages by eliminating income fluctuations caused by unemployment.[3] The bench-

Table 2.1 THE STAGNATION OF FULL-TIME WORKERS' INCOMES AFTER 1973

Men who were 50 in	Their average income at age 50 (1987 dollars)		Growth over previous decade (percent)	
	Census	Adjusted	Census	Adjusted
1946[a]	15,257	15,529	—	—
1956	18,558	19,208	21.6	23.7
1966	23,971	25,168	29.2	31.0
(1973)	(30,578	32,701)	[b]	[b]
1976	30,179	32,752	25.9	30.1
1986	32,960	36,228	9.2	10.6

Source: Income statistics from U.S. Bureau of the Census, *Current Population Reports*, Series P-60, various issues. Income for adjustments from U.S. Department of Commerce, Bureau of Economic Analysis, *National Income and Product Accounts*, various issues. "Average Income of men at 50, Full Time Workers Only" refers to the median income of all male year-round, full-time workers, ages 45–54. Conversion to 1987 dollars made using the Personal Consumption Expenditure (PCE) portion of the GNP deflator.
a. The year 1946 is used as a starting point because it is the first year for which published data are available.
b. As noted in the text, the process of deep stagnation began at the end of 1973 with the first OPEC oil price shock. The growth rate of incomes between 1973 and 1987 on a *per decade basis* was 6.0% (Census) and 8.2% (Adjusted).

mark does have two problems. First, the best source for the benchmark is U.S. census data, and census publications of the 1950s and 1960s did not classify workers by education. As a result, some of the benchmark's growth will reflect the rising educational levels of 45- to 54-year-old men rather than a rising (or falling) wage scale.[4] Second, the census data measure only cash income while it excludes the value of fringe benefits. In recent years, these fringe benefits have become a rising portion of compensation. For this reason table 2.1 contains two columns: income as published by the census and census income figures with approximate adjustments for fringe benefits.[5]

During the 1950s and 1960s labor productivity was growing at 2.5 to 3.5 percent per year and the extra output provided the margin for higher wages. In 1946, for example, the average 50-year-old man working full time had income of $15,257. (Table 2.1: all numbers are adjusted to 1987 dollars). This benchmark rose steadily so that by 1973, the year which ended with the first OPEC oil price increase, the average 50-year-old man who worked full time had income of $30,578.

Relatively little of the earnings gain reflected men's movement out of "bad" jobs into "good" jobs.[6] There was some change in men's occupational structure, particularly in the movement of labor out of low wage agriculture. But the gains reported in table 2.1 reflected rising earnings in all industries. For example, in 1969, a skilled blue collar worker earned about $20,000 (in 1987 dollars), more on average than a typical manager had earned in 1949. But after 1973, income growth slowed dramatically.

At the end of 1973, the fourfold increase in the price of oil led immediately to both recession and inflation. By 1975 the census benchmark had fallen by about 3 percent.[7] More important, 1973 marked the beginning of the sharp slowdown in the growth of productivity.[8]

The income loss from the 1973–1974 oil price shock followed by slow-growing productivity meant that the benchmark did not regain its 1973 level until 1979. Then the Iranian revolution, followed by the Iran-Iraq War, triggered the second round of major OPEC oil price increases and the cycle began again. Between 1973 and 1986, the benchmark grew by only 6.0 percent per decade, compared to 20 to 30 percent per decade in the 1950s and 1960s. Total compensation increased faster than earnings per se as employers paid higher social security taxes and health insurance premiums. But when the benchmark is adjusted for these benefits, it grew by 8.2 percent per decade between 1973 and 1987, less than one-third of its earlier growth rate.

The cessation of wage growth was important because fast rising real wages—and through them rising living standards—had become an integral part of American life. Consider, for example, the issue of the "vanishing middle class." All observers agree that the 1950s and 1960s were decades in which the American middle class was growing. Exactly what did this mean? In casual discussion we think of the middle class as the families in the middle of the income distribution. So a growing middle class suggests greater income equality, with more families bunched near the middle of the income distribution.

When we look at the data, however, we find that income equality did not increase substantially in the 1950s and 1960s.[9] Rather, the middle class was increasing because incomes were growing. In 1947, the average family had income of about $15,000 (in 1987 dollars). By 1969, the average family had income of about $29,000. Family income equality had improved modestly but, more important, *the whole income distribution was shifting to higher levels,*[10] and growing proportions of families were able to afford a single family house, a car (or two cars), a washer, a dryer, and the other pieces of a middle class lifestyle. After 1973, wage growth stopped and family income growth followed. In 1986 median family income stood at $30,670, only 6 percent higher than in 1973. It was in the context of this stagnation that the vanishing middle class became an issue.[11] (The vanishing middle class also has a demographic element, to which we return in chapter 4.)

In a similar fashion, rising real wages were an important part of the assumption that each generation lives better than its parents lived. Consider the example of an 18-year-old man who is getting ready to leave home for college. As he leaves, he looks at his father's salary and what it buys and he keeps the memory as a personal yardstick. In the 1950s and 1960s, the young man would have quickly measured up. By the time he was 30, he would have been earning about 15 percent more, in real terms, than he saw his father earn 12 years earlier.[12] The young man would have known early in his career that he could live as well as he had seen his parents live. In 1986 (after 13 years of slow wage growth), a young man of 30 earned about 15 percent *less* than his father earned 12 years earlier and it is an easy next step to say, as many have, that this is the first generation that will not live as well as their parents (Moynihan 1987). (We present estimates of father and son lifetime income comparisons in chapter 6.)

The growth of real wages also helped to cushion the loss of "good jobs" that occurs even in periods of strong economic growth.[13] The loss of a good job often results in taking a different job at lower pay (for example, Horvath 1987). When real wages are growing throughout the economy, a worker can imagine regaining his old real wage in a few years and relative earnings declines do not lead to absolute earnings declines, at least in the long run. But when real wages are stagnant, absolute earnings declines (and the permanent loss of "good jobs") are far more likely. We look at the issue of good and bad jobs in greater detail in the next chapter.

Wage stagnation also helps to explain the deficits and low savings rates that are one focus of our book. Consider the origins of the federal deficit. When Ronald Reagan assumed office, the country had lived through 7 years of stagnant wages, a sharp break from the previous 27 years in which rising incomes appeared to be automatic. Stagnant wages created enormous pressure both to cut taxes (which put more money in our pockets) and not to cut expenditures (which would have taken money out of our pockets). The resulting federal budget deficit was a way to keep consumption growing in the face of stagnant wages. At the household level, lower savings rates were likewise a way of reconciling ambitious consumption aspirations with income that was growing only slowly.

In the long view of U.S. economic history, the period from the end of World War II through 1973 was unusual for its relative tranquility and its sustained income growth. During this time, Americans experienced steadily rising living standards with the benefits described above: the sense that the middle class was expanding, young people's certainty that they would live better than their parents, and so on. In this context, the post-1973 stagnation of worker's incomes could have been expected to come as an enormous shock to the country.

There was a shock,[14] but it was smaller than one might have expected. Income per capita, the most widely used measure of living standards, helps explain the reason. It was growing strongly even though individual wage rates were not. The census reports that between 1973 and 1986, the median income of all men who worked year round and full time declined from $27,490 to $26,926 (minus 2 percent) while the comparable figure for women rose from $15,553 to $17,147 (plus 10 percent). Over the same period, the census measure of income per capita (i.e. census-defined income per man, woman, and child) rose briskly from $9,926 to $12,250 (plus 22 percent). As noted in chapter 1, census data measure pre-tax, money receipts (excluding capital gains). But disposable income per capita, which corrects for taxes paid, capital gains and noncash income, rose almost as much (21 percent) over the period.

The divergent trends in income per worker and income per capita can be reconciled by noting the substantial increase in the proportion of the population who worked. In 1973, the civilian labor force represented 42 percent of the entire U.S. population including the armed forces. By 1986, the labor force represented 50 percent of the entire population.[15] This increase in relative labor supply was the result of three factors: increases in women's labor force participation, the entrance of the largest baby-boom cohorts into the workforce (as they entered their late teenage years and early 20s), and sustained low birth rates throughout the period.

For individuals, these changes meant a sharp move away from "1950s families" with one paycheck and two or three children. Families in the 1980s typically had two paychecks and one or two children. And a sharp rise in the median age of first marriage increased the number of persons who remained outside families and had only themselves to support.[16]

For the economy as a whole, the changes meant that income per capita (per man, woman, and child) could keep rising despite stagnant income per worker because a growing proportion of the population was at work.[17]

To what extent were smaller families and increased women's labor force participation responses to stagnant earnings? The answer is far from clear. We know that women's labor force participation had been increasing steadily since the 1950s and the baby boom ended in 1964, both well before the onset of stagnation (e.g. Butz and Ward 1979). At the same time, each of the two trends is consistent with income growth that fails to satisfy consumption aspirations, and both trends might have leveled off sooner in an environment of strong wage growth (Elster and Kamlet 1987). Self-reported explanations of behavior are, of course, treacherous because people often see themselves as behaving normally—e.g. having a normal number of children—while the norms themselves change sharply over time.

What *is* clear is that demographic shifts are not a mechanism for continued increases in living standards. Today, about two-thirds of young husband-wife couples begin married life with both partners working. At the same time, the birth rate has stopped falling while the median age of first marriage has stopped increasing. This combination of trends places limits on further increases in the proportion of the population at work and they underline what is simply common sense: Whatever their short-run divergence, income per capita can ultimately grow no faster than income per worker.

Notes

Earlier versions of some of the material in chapters 2 and 3 have appeared in Levy (1988b) and Frank Levy, "Recent Trends in U.S. Earnings and Incomes," in National Bureau of Economic Research, *1989 Macroeconomic Manual*, MIT Press, 1990.

1. Real wages refer to money wages adjusted for inflation, i.e. purchasing power.

2. The competitive spirit in this description reflects the fact that both authors grew up in New York State.

3. Our actual interest is in earnings rather than total money income (which includes earnings as well as unemployment compensation, rents, interest payments, etc.). But table 2.1 is based on published census data which did not include data on earnings per se in the 1950s or 1960s. Table 2.1 refers to men who worked year round and full time, so most of their income is in fact earnings.

4. We use the term rising wage scale to describe a situation in which workers of a given age, education, etc. are paid higher hourly compensation than workers of the same age, education, etc. earned at an earlier time.

5. These corrections are made by inflating census estimates of median individual income by the ratio of other labor income (which includes employer contributions for private fringe benefits) to wage and salary income where both figures are taken from the national income and product accounts.

6. We examine the "good jobs"–"bad jobs" issue in chapter 3.

7. Average earnings for all 50-year-old men (as distinct from full time workers) fell more sharply because unemployment rose sharply in the 1974–1975 recession.

8. While the oil price increase coincided with the productivity slowdown, it was only one of several causes of that slowdown. For a good recent summary of what is known, see Baily and Chakrabarti (1988).

9. In 1949, for example, the middle three-fifths of families received 52.7 percent of all family income. In 1969, the middle three-fifths of families received 53.8 percent of all family income—an increase but not a particularly large one. More generally, people compare their incomes to those of their peers and so don't really know where they stand in the national income distribution.

10. That is, we saw the 50 percent inequality between $30,000 and $20,000 rather than the 50 percent inequality between $15,000 and $10,000.

11. Published census statistics report a slight *decline* in median family incomes between 1973 and 1986. This reflects use of the Consumer Price Index deflator which, analysts agree, overstated inflation by about 6 percent between 1973 and 1982. (The Bureau of Labor Statistics changed its calculation of the Consumer Price Index to deal with these problems in 1982.) We avoid any discontinuity problems by using the personal consumption expenditure (CPE) portion of the GNP deflator.

12. As suggested in table 2.1, the father would have been earning more, too.

13. This is one outcome of what Joseph Schumpeter described as creative destruction. See Schumpeter (1942, chapter 8).

14. One can argue, for example, that one cause of the late 1970s taxpayer revolt was the tension between stagnant incomes and growing government expenditures. But idiosyncratic conditions in various states also played important roles (see Levy 1979).

15. See, for example, U.S. Council of Economic Advisers 1989, tables B-31 and B-32. Note that the figures refer to the ratio of the labor force to the entire population rather than the population aged 16 and over which is used in the computation of labor force participation rates.

16. In 1970, the median age of first marriage was 21 for women and 23 for men. By 1986, the median age of first marriage had risen by about two years for each group (U.S. Bureau of the Census, 1987a).

17. During this period, the United States also increased its living standards through foreign borrowing but census income statistics are not a good device for measuring this increase. As a rough approximation, foreign borrowing permitted the federal government to sharply reduce taxes and run budget deficits without forcing drastic reductions in the rate of gross investment. Because census income statistics are measured on a pretax basis, they do not capture the increase in disposable income that comes from reduced taxes. Bureau of Economic Analysis measures of disposable income per capita (which show a similar percentage growth over the period) do not suffer from this problem. For a discussion of foreign borrowing and living standards, see Litan, Lawrence and Schultze (1988), chapters 1 and 2.

Chapter Three

DETAILED EARNINGS TRENDS AND THE GOOD JOBS–BAD JOBS CONTROVERSY

The statistics in table 2.1 of chapter 2 tell a clear story but are not the numbers that appear in public debate. What is debated publicly, and with some heat, is the proposition that the economy no longer creates middle-class (or "good") jobs, a term that has at least two definitions. A middle-class job can be one that pays enough to support a middle-class living standard, which today includes a single-family home, one or two cars, and so on. Alternatively, a middle-class job can be one that generates income in the middle of the earnings distribution. On this second definition, rising inequality means fewer middle-class jobs, even if all workers' earnings are growing in absolute terms.[1]

EARNINGS DISTRIBUTIONS FOR MEN AND WOMEN: WHY THE SHIFTS?

Figure 3.1 displays the annual earnings distributions of prime age men (ages 25 to 55) for 1973, the last pre-stagnation year, and 1986. The data are taken from the Current Population Survey and the sample consists of men who worked at least one hour during the year. The data are expressed in 1987 dollars.

Had real wages grown at, say, 2 percent per year after 1973, the 1986 distribution in figure 3.1 would have been centered in the $30,000–$40,000 range. In the absence of such growth (see table 2.1, above) the 1973 and 1986 distributions overlap to a substantial degree. When 1973 and 1986 are compared, the proportion of men earning less than $20,000 and the proportion earning more than $50,000 have both increased, while the proportion of men earning $20,000–$50,000 has declined. These changes in the distribution of

Figure 3.1 EARNINGS DISTRIBUTION OF MEN AGES 25–55: 1973, 1986

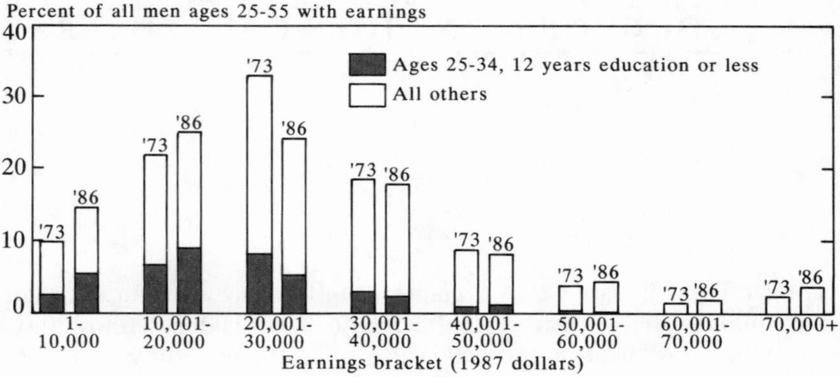

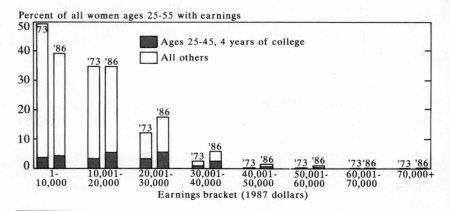

Source: Authors' tabulations from March CPS microdata files.

Figure 3.2 EARNINGS DISTRIBUTION OF WOMEN AGES 25–55: 1973, 1986

Source: Authors' tabulations from March CPS microdata files.

male earnings are consistent with a decline of "good" jobs under both definitions of middle-class jobs. They reflect a declining proportion of workers who earn enough to support a middle-class standard of living (i.e., above $20,000) and an increased inequality of earnings, resulting in a smaller "middle-class."[2]

Figure 3.2 compares the 1973 and 1986 annual earnings distributions of prime age women (ages 25–55). Here, quite a different picture emerges. Women's annual earnings lie well below men's, but between 1973 and 1986 the proportion of women earning less than

$10,000 declined substantially while the proportion earning between $20,000 and $50,000 increased.

What Caused the Changes?

In 1986, the Joint Economic Committee of the U.S. Congress published "The Great American Jobs Machine," authored by Barry Bluestone and Bennett Harrison (1986). The authors argued that although the economic expansion of 1982–1984 had created a large number of new jobs, most were in what they defined as the "low wage" category. By their calculations, 58 percent of the net new jobs created between 1979 and 1984 paid less than $7,012 per year (or $7,712 in 1987 dollars). The paper was influential both for the media attention it received and for the way it shaped the debate over the economy's performance. Even their critics presented opposing arguments in the terms chosen by Bluestone and Harrison.[3] In particular, both Bluestone and Harrison, and many of their critics used shifts in the *distribution of real annual earnings* (figures 3.1 and 3.2) to draw inferences about changes in the relative number of *jobs with high hourly wages* ("good jobs").[4] This was, in fact, a big leap of faith because the distribution of annual earnings can be influenced by a number of factors besides wage rates.

One such factor is the composition of the workforce. At a point in time, wage rates tend to rise with experience (holding education constant) and education (holding experience constant). It then follows that a shift in the age and/or educational composition of the workforce can shift the distribution of annual earnings, even if workers of a given age and education earn precisely what their counterparts earned in previous years.

A second factor is hours worked. In popular debate, "good jobs" refer to jobs that pay high hourly wages, but the "good jobs" debate has been based on the distribution of *annual* earnings data, which says nothing about hourly wages. One example of the problems this can cause is the upward trend in working women's annual hours of work, a trend that could raise the distribution of women's annual earnings even if wage rates have not changed.

Finally, macroeconomic events such as unanticipated inflation and changes in the level of productivity can shift the distribution of real annual earnings even when the numbers of persons in particular occupations (steel workers, fast food clerks, professors, and so on) remain the same.

The annual earnings distributions of men and women shown in

figures 3.1 and 3.2 could have been influenced by all of these factors.[5] To begin to disentangle the separate effects, table 3.1 focuses on 1973, 1979, and 1986 mean annual earnings of 25- to 55-year-old year round full-time workers subdivided by sex, age, and selected educational levels (1987 dollars, PCE adjusted). Earnings means are typically increased by a relatively small proportion of very high earners so each mean is accompanied by the proportion of the sample who earn less than $20,000. From 1973 through 1979, the data exhibit the slower earnings growth described in chapter 2. Relationships among the *relative* earnings of different groups also remained stable. From 1979 through 1986, average earnings in the workforce continued to show little growth, but relative earnings began to diverge sharply.

The post-1979 divergence in relative earnings is manifested in three ways. First, women's earnings, while lower than men's, grew faster than men's earnings, particularly after 1979. For example, among year-round full-time workers, ages 25–34, with four years of college, women's annual earnings increased by 13 percent while men's annual earnings declined by 1 percent. A similar pattern holds among women and men of most other ages and educational levels: women's earnings increased while men's declined.

The second pattern involves workers' education. Among workers of a given sex and age, the earnings of the less educated workers usually showed the slowest gains or the biggest declines. For example, among 35- to 44-year-old women who worked year round and full time, the earnings of women with 4 years of college education grew by 13 percent over the period, while the earnings of women with 4 years of high school grew by only 4 percent.[6]

Finally, among all year-round workers of the same sex, the earnings of young, less educated workers grew less or declined more than the earnings of all other groups.

The gradual convergence of men's and women's earnings has been examined by a number of authors, including Smith and Ward (1984) and Fuchs (1988). The standard demonstration of this convergence is based on the ratio of published median incomes of all women to all men who work year round and full time, a ratio that has grown from .57 in 1973 to .60 in 1979 to .65 in 1986 (U.S. Bureau of the Census 1987b). Because women who work year round and full time have increased their hours worked relative to men, the standard demonstration is overstated. But the data in table 3.1 demonstrate convergence even when hours are controlled.

The growing earnings gap between more and less educated workers

Table 3.1 CHANGES IN MEAN INDIVIDUAL EARNINGS FOR MEN AND WOMEN WHO WORK FULL TIME, BY AGE AND SELECTED EDUCATIONAL LEVEL: 1973, 1979, 1986

	Mean annual earnings (1987 dollars) (percentage earning $20,000 or less)			Percent change in earnings	
	1973	1979	1986	1973–1979	1973–1986
MEN, 25–34					
4 yrs. H.S.	26,364 (27.0)	24,701 (36.0)	22,226 (47.5)	–6	–16
4 yrs. col.	32,036 (14.7)	29,062 (23.6)	31,745 (22.7)	–9	–1
MEN, 35–44					
4 yrs. H.S.	29,736 (19.0)	28,992 (24.5)	27,738 (28.4)	–3	–7
4 yrs. col.	43,331 (9.3)	40,555 (11.8)	40,194 (13.2)	–6	–7
MEN, 45–54					
4 yrs. H.S.	30,621 (19.8)	29,773 (23.5)	29,520 (24.2)	–3	–4
4 yrs. col.	45,757 (8.4)	43,565 (10.9)	45,973 (11.5)	–5	+ <.5

continued

Table 3.1 CHANGES IN MEAN INDIVIDUAL EARNINGS FOR MEN AND WOMEN WHO WORK FULL TIME, BY AGE AND SELECTED EDUCATIONAL LEVEL: 1973, 1979, 1986 (continued)

WOMEN, 25–34					
4 yrs. H.S.	15,157 (83.1)	15,516 (81.0)	15,700 (77.0)	+2	+4
4 yrs. col.	20,733 (47.9)	20,116 (57.8)	23,333 (43.7)	−3	+13
WOMEN, 35–44					
4 yrs. H.S.	16,006 (77.4)	15,963 (78.7)	17,373 (69.3)	−<.5	+9
4 yrs. col.	23,283 (41.1)	21,391 (51.4)	26,214 (34.5)	−8	+13
WOMEN, 45–54					
4 yrs. H.S.	16,406 (77.3)	16,456 (76.6)	17,400 (67.2)	+<.5	+6
4 yrs. col.	23,075 (39.3)	21,549 (51.4)	25,001 (30.8)	−7	+8

Source: Authors' tabulations of March CPS microdata files.

has been less studied and is a reversal of past developments. In 1976 Richard Freeman in *The Overeducated American* highlighted the falling rate of return on a college diploma. In Freeman's description, America had reached a state of over-education in which:

> ... the economic rewards to college education are markedly lower than has historically been the case and/or in which additional investment in college training will drive down those rewards—a society in which education has become, like investments in other mature industries or activities a marginal rather than highly profitable endeavor. (Freeman 1976, 4–5)

Published census data supported Freeman's view. Consider the behavior over time of the ratio of median income of 25- to 34-year-old men with 4 years of college to the median income of 25- to 34-year-old men with 4 years of high school.[7] Throughout the 1950s the ratio stood at about 1.3, that is, the college man earned 30 percent more than the high school man. By the end of the 1960s the increasing proportion of college graduates had caused the ratio to fall to 1.25. And by 1973, roughly the time Freeman was writing, it had fallen to 1.15. The ratio remained between 1.15 and 1.2 for the rest of the 1970s. But then, as we have seen, the ground began to shift, most clearly under younger men (table 3.1). Among 25- to 34-year-old men, the ratio grew to 1.30 in 1980 (a recession year) and kept increasing, reaching 1.5 in 1986.[8]

Together, the data in tables 2.1 and 3.1 begin to suggest a two-part story behind post-1973 earnings changes and their impact on middle-class jobs. The first part is the combination of oil-price shocks and slow productivity growth, which together slowed the rate of real wage growth for all workers. The second part is the shifts in the demand for and the supply of different kinds of labor, which caused the earnings of some workers to grow faster than average and the earnings of other workers to grow more slowly. What remains to be determined is the relative importance of supply and demand shifts in this story.

Changes in Supply and Demand

We begin to look at this question in table 3.2, which goes beyond table 3.1 by looking at the 1973 and 1986 mean earnings of all men and women, ages 25–55, who worked at least one hour for pay during the year. For comparison, table 3.2 reproduces from table 3.1 the percentage change in earnings for the subset of workers who worked year round and full time.

Table 3.2 MEAN EARNINGS OF ALL MEN AND WOMEN WITH $1 OR MORE OF EARNINGS: 1973, 1986

	Mean annual earnings (1987 dollars) (percent earning $20,000 or less)		Percent change in earnings, all workers	Percent change in earnings for subset of year-round full-time workers (from table 3.1)
	1973	1986		
MEN, 25–34				
4 yrs. H.S.	24,267 (35.7)	19,410 (60.2)	−20	−16
4 yrs. col.	28,339 (27.7)	29,170 (32.5)	+3	−1
MEN, 35–44				
4 yrs. H.S.	27,946 (25.5)	25,103 (41.8)	−11	−7
4 yrs. col.	41,926 (12.8)	38,374 (20.1)	−8	−7
MEN, 45–54				
4 yrs. H.S.	28,102 (28.6)	27,133 (37.9)	−3	−4
4 yrs. col.	42,988 (14.7)	43,803 (18.4)	+2	+<.5

WOMEN, 25–34				
4 yrs. H.S.	9,870 (94.9)	11,133 (89.9)	+13	+4
4 yrs. col.	14,876 (78.1)	18,850 (64.1)	+27	+13
WOMEN, 35–44				
4 yrs. H.S.	10,926 (92.2)	12,440 (85.8)	+14	+9
4 yrs. col.	14,878 (80.1)	19,837 (62.3)	+33	+27
WOMEN, 45–54				
4 yrs. H.S.	12,223 (91.1)	13,220 (85.1)	+8	+6
4 yrs. col.	18,835 (72.0)	19,753 (59.5)	+5	+3

Source: Authors' tabulations of March CPS microdata files.

Earnings patterns for all workers follow earnings patterns for year round full-time workers, with slightly larger swings. Where the earnings of year-round full-time workers increased, as is the case for college educated women, the earnings for all workers with the same characteristics increased at a faster rate. Where the earnings of year-round full-time workers declined, as is the case for young, high school educated men, the earnings of all workers in the same group declined at a greater rate. The fact that a group's wages and its hours of work were moving in the same direction suggests that relative wage movements were driven primarily by shifts in demand for different kinds of labor.[9]

Table 3.3 addresses the issue of supply and demand more directly by comparing changes in a group's mean annual earnings with changes in the group's size. These data also point to the importance of demand shifts in relative earnings movements. Among men or women of a given age, between 1973 and 1986 the number of college educated

Table 3.3 CHANGES IN GROUP'S SIZE AND GROUP'S AVERAGE ANNUAL EARNINGS FOR 25- TO 55-YEAR-OLD MEN AND WOMEN WORKERS: 1973, 1986

	Number of workers		Percent change in group size	Percent change in annual earnings
	1973	1986		
	(millions)			
MEN, 25–34				
4 yrs. H.S.	5.1	8.1	+58	−20
4 yrs. col.	1.8	3.3	+83	+3
MEN, 35–44				
4 yrs. H.S.	3.8	5.3	+39	−11
4 yrs. col.	1.1	2.6	+136	−8
MEN, 45–54				
4 yrs. H.S.	4.0	3.8	−5	−3
4 yrs. col.	1.1	1.2	+9	+2
WOMEN, 25–34				
4 yrs. H.S.	3.5	6.7	+91	+13
4 yrs. col.	1.1	3.0	+172	+27
WOMEN, 35–44				
4 yrs. H.S.	2.8	5.8	+107	+14
4 yrs. col.	.5	1.7	+240	+33
WOMEN, 45–54				
4 yrs. H.S.	3.0	4.0	+33	+8
4 yrs. col.	.4	.8	+100	+5

Source: Authors' tabulations of March 1974 and March 1987 CPS microdata files.

workers grew more quickly than the number of high school educated workers, but high school workers' earnings grew more slowly. Similarly, among workers of a given age and education, the number of working women grew more rapidly than the number of working men, but women's mean earnings increased while men's mean earnings declined or, in a few cases, remained constant.

In sum, shifts in demand were not responsible for *absolute* earnings gains and losses; oil price shocks and the productivity slowdown were the principal culprits here. But shifts in demand did play an important role in relative earnings gains and losses, and explain why some groups did better than average while others did worse.

To understand shifts in demand during the 1970s and 1980s we need to examine the distribution of workers across industries in the early 1970s. For ease of exposition we have collapsed industries into four groups:

☐ Durable and non-durable manufacturing;
☐ Mining and construction;
☐ Agriculture;
☐ The service sector, including wholesale and retail trade; finance, insurance, and real estate; personal services; business and professional services; transportation, utilities, and communication; and public administration.

Table 3.4 shows the 1973 distribution of men and women across these employment categories. For men only, we include persons who were not employed during the year.[10] In 1973, less educated men were concentrated in durable manufacturing and other goods producing industries, while more educated men and women were concentrated in services. Among men with a high school education or less, for example, about 45 percent were employed in durable manufacturing or other goods industries while about 40 percent were employed in the service sector. Among men with at least some college education, about 60 percent were employed in the service sector. Among women, the proportion employed in the service sector ran from 54 percent (for women who had not graduated high school) to 97 percent (for women with more than four years of college). It follows, then, that any decrease in manufacturing employment would disproportionately affect less educated men.

Such a decrease in manufacturing employment did indeed take place between 1973 and 1986. Manufacturing, especially durable manufacturing, is sensitive to economic downturns, and after 1973

Table 3.4 DISTRIBUTION OF MEN AND WOMEN ACROSS INDUSTRIAL
SECTORS, 1973

	Manufg.	Mining and construct.	Service sector	Agri.	Persons who did not work
ALL MEN, 25–55, BY EDUCATION					
Less than H.S.	.32	.16	.35	.07	.10
H.S. Grad.	.32	.12	.48	.04	.04
1–3 yrs. col.	.26	.08	.59	.02	.05
4 yrs. col.	.24	.06	.65	.02	.03
4+ yrs. col.	.14	.02	.80	.01	.03
WOMEN, 25–55, BY EDUCATION					
Less than H.S.	.35	.01	.54	.09	n/a
H.S. Grad.	.20	.02	.76	.02	n/a
1–3 yrs. col.	.12	.01	.86	.01	n/a
4 yrs. col.	.06	.02	.91	.01	n/a
4+ yrs. col.	.02	.01	.97	.00	n/a

Source: Authors' tabulations of March 1974 CPS microdata files.
n/a = not applicable. Data for women exclude persons who did not work during the
year. See text for explanation.

two sharp downturns hurt employment: the recessions of 1973–1975
and 1980–1982 (Lawrence 1982). But job openings in manufacturing
continued to be reduced after the second recession because the post-
1982 recovery was accompanied by an overvalued dollar that further
undercut both foreign and domestic demand for U.S. manufactured
goods.

Table 3.5 compares the 1973, 1979, and 1986 industrial employment distributions of men and women. Among 25- to 34-year-olds
with a high school education, between 1973 and 1986 the proportion
in manufacturing fell sharply from 34 to 24 percent with most of the
drop coming after 1979. Conversely, among 25- to 34-year-old men
with 4 years of college, the proportion of college educated men in
manufacturing held steady at 20 percent. The comparison is note-
worthy because the absolute number of college educated men in this
age group grew faster than the number of high school educated men
(table 3.3). This suggests that younger men were losing manufacturing jobs not only because of the slow growth of manufacturing employment, but because the composition of that employment was
shifting toward more educated workers.

In theory, the shift of younger, less educated men out of goods

Table 3.5 DISTRIBUTION OF MEN AND WOMEN ACROSS INDUSTRIAL
SECTORS, BY SELECTED AGE AND EDUCATION: 1973, 1979, 1986
(percent)

		Manufg.	Other goods industries	Service sector	Agri.	Persons who did not work
MEN, 25–34						
H.S. Grad.	1973	.34	.14	.46	.03	.03
	1979	.32	.14	.44	.03	.06
	1986	.24	.17	.48	.04	.07
4 yrs. col.	1973	.20	.06	.68	.02	.04
	1979	.20	.07	.66	.03	.04
	1986	.20	.06	.70	.02	.02
MEN, 35–44						
H.S. Grad.	1973	.32	.12	.49	.04	.03
	1979	.31	.15	.46	.04	.05
	1986	.27	.14	.48	.03	.08
4 yrs. col.	1973	.28	.05	.64	.02	.01
	1979	.22	.06	.66	.02	.03
	1986	.23	.06	.67	.02	.02
MEN, 45–55						
H.S. Grad.	1973	.29	.10	.50	.05	.06
	1979	.28	.13	.48	.04	.06
	1986	.28	.13	.48	.04	.07
4 yrs. col.	1973	.26	.08	.60	.02	.04
	1979	.28	.05	.62	.01	.03
	1986	.27	.06	.63	.01	.03
WOMEN, 25–34						
H.S. Grad.	1973	.23	.02	.72	.03	n/a
	1979	.21	.18	.76	.01	n/a
	1986	.17	.01	.80	.01	n/a
4 yrs. col.	1973	.05	.01	.93	.01	n/a
	1979	.09	.01	.90	.01	n/a
	1986	.11	.02	.86	.01	n/a
WOMEN, 35–44						
H.S. Grad.	1973	.18	.01	.79	.02	n/a
	1979	.18	.02	.78	.02	n/a
	1986	.16	.02	.81	.01	n/a
4 yrs. col.	1973	.03	<.5%	.96	.01	n/a
	1979	.07	.01	.92	.01	n/a
	1986	.07	.01	.91	.01	n/a

continued

Table 3.5 DISTRIBUTION OF MEN AND WOMEN ACROSS INDUSTRIAL
SECTORS, BY SELECTED AGE AND EDUCATION: 1973, 1979, 1986
(percent) (continued)

		Manufg.	Other goods industries	Service sector	Agri.	Persons who did not work
WOMEN, 45–55						
H.S. Grad.	1973	.19	.01	.77	.03	n/a
	1979	.18	.02	.79	.02	n/a
	1986	.17	.01	.79	.03	n/a
4 yrs. col.	1973	.04	.01	.94	.01	n/a
	1979	.05	.02	.92	.02	n/a
	1986	.06	<.5%	.93	.01	n/a

Source: Authors' tabulations of March 1974, March 1980, and March 1987 CPS microdata files. CPS public use sample.
n/a = not applicable. Data for women exclude persons who did not work during the year. See text for explanation.

production might have been a voluntary response to more attractive alternatives in other sectors. In reality, average manufacturing earnings outpaced service sector industries by a higher amount in 1986 than in 1973. Thus, a more plausible explanation for the shift is that the contraction of manufacturing employment placed young, less educated men in a position of excess supply. Service sector industries absorbed some of this excess supply but at the cost of a steep decline in relative earnings, which led to a sharpened earnings distinction between the manufacturing and service sectors.[11] More generally, the movement of younger, less educated men out of manufacturing did not result in more service sector employment for this group. Instead, it moved more young men out of the labor force. The earnings statistics in tables 3.1 and 3.2 exclude men who do not work during the year, but the existence of such men also points to their being in excess supply. The result was a sharp decline in the earnings of young, less educated men in all sectors, including manufacturing.[12]

Macroeconomic forces were not the only factor in these observed wage patterns. Since 1980, productivity within manufacturing has revived to a reasonable degree while productivity in services has remained stagnant. The difference between these rates has created a situation in which manufacturing has had relatively lower labor demand. At the same time, Blackburn, Bloom and Freeman (1990) present evidence showing that the wages of less educated workers have been independently affected by a decline in unionization.

When compared to young, less educated men, between 1973 and 1986 other groups of workers were in relatively stronger positions. Older, less educated men had the benefit of job seniority, while better educated men and most women were heavily concentrated in the service sector, so were relatively insulated from the problems of manufacturing.[13] Better educated women also benefited from moderate occupational mobility (Bianchi and Spain 1986).

Had average wages continued to grow throughout the economy, young high school educated men could have lost ground *relative* to college educated men but still have been in absolute terms better off than the high school workers of 15 years ago. But during the post-1973 stagnation, *relative* losses became *absolute* losses as well.

Did these economic changes have a differential effect by race? Table 3.6 provides a partial answer to this question by examining the earnings of 25- to 55-year-old black and white men, grouped by selected educational levels.

In the 1950s and 1960s the earnings of black and white men grew moderately closer.[14] Since 1973, this trend has continued but at a very slow rate. The ratio of the average black male's earnings to the average white male's earnings rose from 64 percent in 1973 to 68 percent in 1986 (calculated from table 3.6 figures). The detailed earnings figures in table 3.6 show that this convergence was concentrated among older men (particularly those with 4 years of college). The earnings of college educated black men ages 45–54 rose from 59 percent of their white counterparts' earnings in 1973 to 68 percent in 1986. Among 25- to 34- year old men, however, black high school graduates had larger earnings declines (25 percent) than white high school graduates (20 percent) and black men with 4 years of college saw earnings declines (14 percent) while white men with 4 years of college saw small earnings gains (3 percent).

Within this stagnation, earnings inequality *among* black men has grown (figure 3.3). For 25- to 55-year-old black men with earnings, the proportion earning below $10,000 and the proportion earning above $30,000 have both increased between 1973 and 1986, while the proportion earning between $10,000 and $30,000 declined. Earnings inequality among white men also grew, but did so based on a higher average (figure 3.4).

In sum, a resolution of the "good jobs—bad jobs" debate must make three points. First, the slow growth of earnings, a macroeconomic

Table 3.6 MEAN EARNINGS OF BLACK AND WHITE MEN WITH $1 OR MORE OF EARNINGS: 1973, 1986

	Black men Earnings (1987 dollars)			White men Earnings (1987 dollars)		
	1973	1986	Percent change	1973	1986	Percent change
ALL MEN, 25–55[a]	18,595	19,608	+5	29,267	29,040	−1
AGE 25–34						
4 yrs. H.S.	19,726	14,723	−25	25,242	20,172	−20
4 yrs. col.	25,571	22,081	−14	28,880	29,869	+3
AGE 35–44						
4 yrs. H.S.	21,296	18,351	−14	29,096	26,010	−11
4 yrs. col.	27,399	28,100	+3	42,833	39,492	−8
AGE 45–54						
4 yrs. H.S.	20,308	20,551	+1	29,740	27,797	−7
4 yrs. col.	26,634	30,768	+16	44,951	45,193	+2

Source: Authors' tabulations of March CPS microdata files.
a. Includes all male earners, ages 25–55, of any educational level.

Figure 3.3 EARNINGS DISTRIBUTION OF BLACK MEN: 1973, 1986

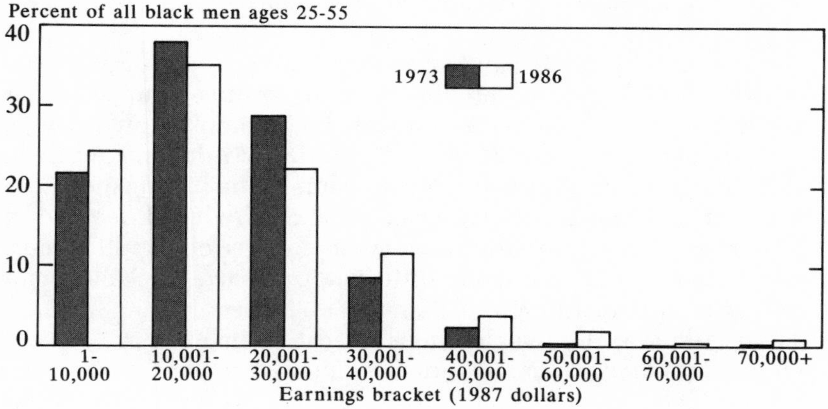

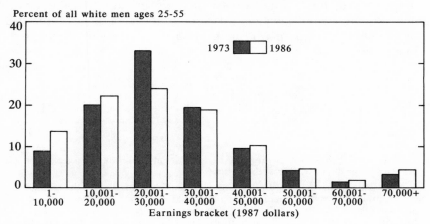

Source: Authors' tabulations from March CPS microdata files.

Figure 3.4 EARNINGS DISTRIBUTION OF WHITE MEN: 1973, 1986

Source: Authors' tabulations from March CPS microdata files.

phenomenon, affected earnings in all sectors. Today, young persons with four years of college working at what used to be called a good white collar job for $25,000 must wonder whether they will ever be able to afford a house like the one in which they grew up. In this sense, weak productivity growth and the income losses of oil price shocks have limited the number of jobs with "middle-class pay-checks" and have helped create a wide audience for the "good jobs–bad jobs" debate.

Second, the shift in demand away from young, less educated male workers resulted in fewer job opportunities for this group at higher wage levels. In 1973, 64 percent of male high school graduates, ages 25–34, earned more than $20,000 per year (in 1987 dollars). By 1986, this proportion had declined to 40 percent. Shifts in demand occur all the time, of course, but as we noted above, reduced demand in a context of general stagnation has much more serious implications. In 1986, for example, about one-fifth of all prime age black men *with earnings* reported earning less than $10,000 a year (figure 3.3).

Finally, the "good jobs–bad jobs" debate is more a story about men (in particular, young, less educated men) than women. Between 1973 and 1986 women's earnings have been systematically below those of men, but the proportion of women earning more than $20,000 per year rose from 16 percent in 1973 to 27 percent in 1986. A large part of this increase reflects increased hours of work, but some part reflects rising real wages. Among younger women there is some evidence of growing inequality between more and less educated workers. But on the whole, women's position in the labor market improved moderately over this period both in absolute terms and relative to men.

Notes

1. That is, while all earnings are growing, earnings at the top of the distribution are growing faster than earnings at the bottom.

2. This issue was prominent in the 1988 presidential campaign and the search for a cause surfaced in many forms including Michael Dukakis's references to "Good Jobs at Good Wages" and "Two-Paycheck Prosperity," Richard Gephardt's commercial featuring the "$48,000 K-Car" (the tariff-driven cost of a moderately priced American car in Japan), Jesse Jackson's speeches on the victims of "economic violence," and Pat Robertson's speeches to South Carolina textile workers in which he argued that their industry and their wages were being undermined by international bankers.

3. A sample of critical commentary includes Kosters and Ross (1988), Samuelson (1987), Brookes (1987), and U.S. Council of Economic Advisers (1988). Norwood (1987) is slightly more agnostic. Another article relevant to the debate is Rosenthal (1985).

4. Here and elsewhere in this book, we use the term "wages" to refer to the hourly rate of compensation to any employee, including those whose pay is contracted on a weekly, monthly, or annual basis.

5. The distributions in figures 3.1 and 3.2 differ in two major respects from the distributions used by both sides of the "good jobs" debate. Where we focus on 25- to 55-year-old workers, those researchers often focus on all workers age 16 and above. Where in figures 3.1 and 3.2 we present the data in $10,000 increments, most authors in the debate simply divide annual earnings into a "low-medium-high" classification. Our age breaks focus attention on adult workers who are full participants in the labor force, eliminating students (<25) and early retirees (>55). The more detailed earnings breaks permit absolute rather than just relative analyses over time.

6. For clarity, the table 3.1 is restricted to persons with exactly 12 or 16 years of education. Tabulations not published here indicate a generally monotonic relationship between earnings changes and education within each age-sex group.

7. We use income statistics rather than earnings per se in this comparison because the census did not publish separate earnings statistics in the 1950s and 1960s.

8. This fact seems to have been discovered more or less independently by Levy and Michel (1987), Sum and Fogg (1987), Murphy and Welch (1988), and Freeman (personal communication, 1989).

9. Ideally, one would verify this fact by directly tabulating annual hours worked. Unfortunately, the 1973 Current Population Survey only contains data on hours normally worked per week (a continuous variable) and weeks worked per year (a classified variable). Among people who work only part of the year, weeks worked are coded in broad classes, e.g., 27–39 weeks, which means that annual hours of work cannot be estimated with precision.

10. Later in this chapter we will compare industrial distributions for women in 1973 and 1986. Women's labor force participation increased sharply during this period, making it hard to separate industrial shifts from increased work effort. For this reason, we confine women's industrial distributions to working women who worked at some point during the year.

11. Earnings in the service sector industries of transportation, communications, and utilities also dropped as a result of deregulation.

12. A paper by Blackburn, Bloom and Freeman (1990) similarly concludes that declining earnings among young, less educated men is much more a function of wage declines within industries than the result of employment shifts from higher to lower wage industries.

13. Though it appears from tables 3.4 and 3.5 that young, less educated women faced some of the same pressure from manufacturing as young, less educated men.

14. See, for example, Levy (1988a), chapter 7, and Smith and Welch (1989), p. 522.

Chapter Four

FAMILY INCOME DISTRIBUTION

In casual discussion, earnings inequality and family income inequality are often treated interchangeably. In fact, although the two distributions are related, they differ in many respects. Trends in family incomes depend on trends in individual earnings, but they are also linked to the number of earners per family and the amount of income from sources other than earnings, such as interest payments, private pensions, and government transfer payments.

Trends in family incomes also depend on marriage rates. In chapter 2, we noted that the age of first marriage had risen sharply since 1970. Evidence suggests that between 1973 and 1986 those young people who postponed marriage had lower than average earnings.[1] This suggests that the economic experience of many *families* is somewhat better than the economic experience of the population as a whole.

A STORY OF SLOW CHANGES

In the years since World War II, census measures of the U.S. family income distribution have displayed gradual movements around an absolutely level of inequality. Family income equality increased in the 1950s and 1960s. But in 1969, the year of greatest income equality by census measures, the poorest one-fifth of families received 5.6 percent of all family income while the richest one-fifth received 40.6 percent, a ratio of about $1.00 to $7.25. Income inequality increased gradually in the 1970s and increased more sharply in the 1980s so that today the corresponding ratio is $1.00 to $9.60, but as shown in part B of table 4.1, a family did not have to be a millionaire to be in the richest one-fifth of families.[2]

These movements in the U.S. family income distribution are displayed in table 4.1. Over the course of 40 years, the income share

Table 4.1 SHAPE OF U.S. FAMILY INCOME DISTRIBUTION

A. Percent share of all family income going to each fifth of families

	1st fifth (poorest)	2nd fifth	3rd fifth	4th fifth	5th fifth (richest)	total
1949	4.5	11.9	17.3	23.5	42.7	100
1959	4.9	12.3	17.9	23.8	41.1	100
1969	5.6	12.4	17.7	23.7	40.6	100
1979	5.2	11.6	17.5	24.1	41.7	100
1988	4.6	10.7	16.7	24.0	44.0	100

B. 1988 Income Upper Limits for Each Quintile

1st quintile ends at	2nd quintile ends at	3rd quintile ends at	4th quintile ends at
$15,102	$26,182	$38,500	$55,966

Source: U.S. Bureau of the Census (1987b).

going to the poorest quintile of families has varied between 4.5 percent and 5.6 percent, while the income share of the top quintile has varied between 40.6 percent and 44.0 percent. However, the variations in table 4.1 are larger than they appear. Between 1949 and 1988 the income share of the lowest quintile varied at most only 1 percent, but this is a 1 percent range of *all family income* for a group that received only about 5 percent of all family income to begin with. In 1988, for example, an income share of 5.6 percent rather than 4.6 percent would have raised mean income in the lowest quintile by almost $2,000, no small difference.

Figure 4.1 presents a more detailed picture of 1973 and 1986 family income distribution. Here, as in the distribution of prime-age male annual earnings (figure 3.1), there has been little real growth between 1973 and 1986. Over this period median family income increased from $28,890 to $30,670, a far slower rate than in earlier decades. And as in the distribution of male earnings, stagnant family incomes were accompanied by greater inequality. Between 1973 and 1986 the proportions of families with incomes below $10,000 and above $50,000 both increased moderately, while the proportion of families with incomes between $10,000 and $50,000 declined moderately.

Figure 4.1 and the data in table 4.1 raise two questions. First, to what extent do the data support perceptions of a "vanishing middle class"?

Figure 4.1 FAMILY INCOME DISTRIBUTION: 1973, 1986

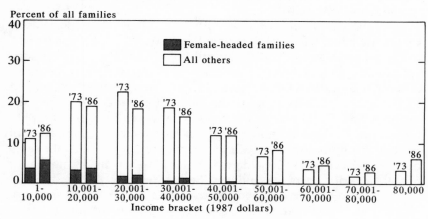

Source: Authors' tabulations from March CPS microdata files.

(Kuttner 1983; Thurow 1984). Second, why has inequality remained relatively constant over 40 years in the face of two developments favoring equality: the declining proportion of families in low-wage agriculture and the improving relative incomes of elderly families?

We can place the issue of the vanishing middle class in perspective by looking at income equality trends in the 1950s and 1960s. These were years when the middle class was rapidly expanding (Gans 1967). Although income equality improved, the improvement was not dramatic. Similarly, family income equality deteriorated during the 1970s and particularly in the 1980s, but the deterioration does not seem large enough to account for fears of a vanishing middle class.[3]

One plausible explanation for these fears is that the post-World War II growth of the American middle class did not reflect reduced inequality (in other words, more families in the middle of the distribution) as much as it reflected rapid income growth. Between 1947 and 1973, median family income rose from $14,830 to $28,890 (36 percent per decade). This growth was accompanied by rapid increases in the proportions of families who owned their own homes, cars, washing machines, dryers, televisions, and the other material elements of a middle-class lifestyle (Levy 1988a, chapter 4). Between 1973 and 1986, median family income only grew from $28,890 to $30,670 (5 percent per decade), and it was this stagnation that helped prompt fears of a vanishing middle class. (There is a second element to fears of a vanishing middle class that involves changes in the kinds of families that occupy various portions of the distribution. We return to this shortly.)

The relative stability of inequality over almost four decades is surprising when one considers post-World War II population trends. In the late 1940s, the bottom quintile of the family income distribution was dominated by two kinds of families: elderly families, many of whom still worked, and farm families, who constituted about 11 percent of all families and who typically reported very low cash incomes.[4] Since that time, rapid gains in agricultural productivity have reduced the need for agricultural labor, and the proportion of families in agriculture has declined from 11 to 2 percent. At the same time, successive cohorts of elderly families have benefited from greater Social Security coverage, indexed Social Security payments (after 1971), and greater private pension coverage. As a result, incomes of elderly families over the last 15 years have grown more rapidly than incomes of non-elderly families (U.S. Council of Economic Advisers 1985; see also table 4.2 below). These events, ceteris paribus, should have increased family income equality, but that did not occur.

A proximate explanation for the family income inequality of recent years is contained in table 4.2. These data show that while the incomes of elderly families were rising, the number of families headed by single women was growing rapidly. Among families with a head under age 65, the proportion headed by a single woman rose from about 1 in 8 in 1973 to 1 in 5 in 1986. In both years the median incomes of such families were well below the incomes of other families in the population. The result was a kind of "swap" in which elderly families moved from the bottom of the income distribution to the lower middle, while their "vacated places" at the bottom were taken by new female-headed families with children.

The data in table 4.2 imply that greater income inequality might have been the joint product of more female-headed families and more two-paycheck families. However, this is not quite correct. Many working wives come from families where the husband's earnings are very low. If, as an exercise, family income inequality were recalculated disregarding all wives' earnings, the resulting inequality would be greater than it actually is.[5]

We noted earlier that population shifts within the income distribution add to perceptions of a vanishing middle class. In particular, the "swap" of female-headed families for elderly families at the bottom of the distribution has led to a situation in which income inequality among families with children has increased substantially (figure 4.2). We saw in chapter 2 that part of the post-1973 increase

Table 4.2 FREQUENCY AND MEDIAN INCOME OF MAJOR FAMILY TYPES: 1973, 1986

Family type	1973		1986	
	Percent of families	Median income (1987 dollars)	Percent of families	Median income (1987 dollars)
All	100	28,890	100	30,670
Family Head ≥ Age 65[a]	14.4	15,956	15.8	20,752
Husband-Wife <65 Wife does not Work	39.7	30,218	24.5	29,787
Husband-Wife <65 Wife Works	33.6	37,158	42.3	38,750
Female Family Head <65	10.3	13,424	14.4	11,308
All Other Families	2.1	—	3.0	—

Source: *Current Population Reports*, various issues. Some medians are interpolated from published data.
a. Includes both male- and female-headed families with head over age 65.

Figure 4.2 DISTRIBUTION OF CHILDREN BY FAMILY INCOME: 1973, 1986

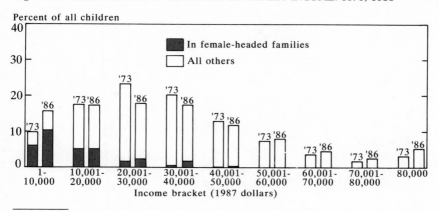

Source: Authors' tabulations from March CPS microdata files.

in per capita income reflected low national birth rates. In this context, a growing proportion of families headed by women led to an even more rapid growth in the percentage of children in female-headed families, from 10 percent of all children in 1973 to 20 percent of all children in 1986. The result has been an increase in the proportion of children in families with incomes under $10,000 (1987 dollars) from 1 in 9 in 1973 to about 1 in 6 in 1986. This process has taken place most rapidly among black families. In 1986, 41 percent of all black families were headed by a single woman under 65 and, as a partial consequence, just over 1 black child in 3 lived in a family with income of less than $10,000 per year (table 4.3 and figure 4.3).

SUMMARY

This shifting of families within the income distribution adds to a sense of increased inequality. The growing number of poor children

Table 4.3 FAMILY STRUCTURES BY RACE: 1973, 1986

	1973		1986	
	Percent of families	Median income (1987 dollars)	Percent of families	Median income (1987 dollars)
Black families				
Head over 65	13	10,123	13	14,107
Husband-Wife <65 Wife Works	31	31,401	34	33,491
Husband-Wife <65 Wife Does Not Work	25	18,881	12	18,972
Female Head >65	31	10,369	41	9,414
	100		100	
White families				
Head over 65	15	15,715	17	21,474
Husband-Wife <65 Wife Works	35	37,848	46	44,883
Husband-Wife <65 Wife Does Not Work	42	31,456	26	30,945
Female Head <65	08	15,532	11	16,320
	100		100	

Source: Estimated from Current Population Reports, various issues.

Figure 4.3 DISTRIBUTION OF BLACK CHILDREN BY FAMILY INCOME: 1973, 1986

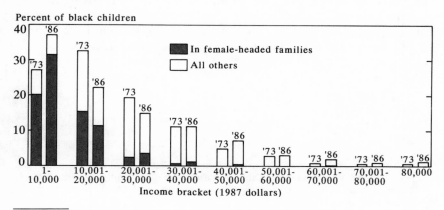

Source: Authors' tabulations from March CPS microdata files.

Figure 4.4 DISTRIBUTION OF WHITE CHILDREN BY FAMILY INCOME: 1973, 1986

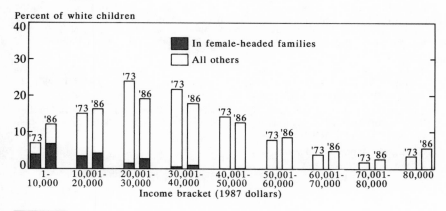

Source: Authors' tabulations from March CPS microdata files.

is highly visible and newsworthy, as it should be. More precisely, poor children are more newsworthy than the improved incomes of the elderly. This leads to a perception that income inequality is rising more significantly than census statistics indicate.

This perception may contain a kernel of truth. If middle-class families are no longer even a small proportion of the bottom of the income distribution, and if low-income female-headed families remain female-headed families for long periods of time (Bane and Ellwood 1986), it may be that mobility *within* the income distribution has declined over the last 15 years, and that a fairly stable distribution of current family incomes obscures a growing inequality of permanent family incomes. We return to this issue later in this book.

Notes

1. In 1986, for example, 56 percent of all men, ages 25–34, were married and had average individual income (excluding the earnings of other family members, etc.) of $24,620; 44 percent of all men, ages 25–34, were not married and had average individual income of $20,087.

2. The best international comparisons of income inequality show that U.S. family income inequality is high not only in absolute terms but also relative to inequality in other countries. For example, Sawyer (1976) shows that the poorest quintile of U.S. *households* received 3.8 percent of pretax income in 1972, compared to 5.4 percent in Germany in 1973, 7.6 percent in Japan in 1969, 4.4 percent in the United Kingdom in 1969, 4.3 percent in Canada in 1969, and so on. More recent work by Coder, Rainwater and Smeeding (1988), which uses data developed by the Luxembourg Income Study, shows that in the 1979–1983 period, the level of disposable income inequality among U.S. families was the highest of the ten industrialized countries in their sample.

3. This is all the more true because most people don't know where they stand in the income distribution, and many families in the top quintile (income over $52,000) still consider themselves as middle class.

4. Cash incomes obviously understate the relative well-being of many farm families, but the purpose of this discussion is to examine trends in reported census (i.e. cash or money income) statistics.

5. Eugene Smolensky, personal communication, 1988.

Chapter Five

FAMILY WEALTH GROWTH

For most families, income is the primary measure of well-being because current consumption is paid for from income flows. But wealth (that is, the sum of assets and liabilities) also plays a major role in determining the financial stability of families.

The purpose of wealth varies considerably among individual families, but most view it as providing some protection against future fluctuations in income or consumption. Fluctuations in income occur because of events such as retirement or unemployment; fluctuations in consumption occur because of planned-for events such as home purchases or children's education, or unplanned-for events such as illness. The greater the wealth of a family, the more securely it is protected against deterioration in its economic status due to unanticipated disasters. Thus, the measure of wealth, and particularly of wealth after deducting debts, becomes an important gauge of the well-being of individual families or groups of families.

DEFINITIONS OF WEALTH

Economists disagree on many aspects of wealth analysis: how to measure it, whether to count as wealth social security and other deferred pension income, even why individuals accumulate wealth in the first place (for instance, do they plan to leave bequests to their heirs?). The decision to include or exclude social security and private pension wealth is particularly controversial and can make a significant difference in the interpretation of wealth trends. Wolff (1989) reports that including both private pensions and social security at present value turns a decline in real per household net wealth between 1969 and 1983 to an increase.[1]

We believe that social security and pension wealth in defined benefit pension plans are not equivalent to wealth holdings controlled directly by individuals. Both are subject to uncertain future payments because of tax and benefit policies and because of questions about the financial viability of some corporate pension funds. At best, they are a restricted asset since they cannot be bequeathed, borrowed against, or transferred. In essence, social security and defined benefit pension programs are more like income entitlements than either liquid or illiquid assets and should be treated in a similar manner. In the case of poor or disabled persons, for example, we would not consider including the present value of future welfare payments in net wealth even though such payments might cause families to alter their economic behavior.

In any case, for the average family, the definition of wealth is straightforward. The single most important component for a home-owning family is the equity in its principal residence. Add to this assets such as savings accounts, stocks and bonds, other real property, interest in a business, art objects, and other material holdings, and one has a conventionally accepted profile of the wealth status of a household. Of course, total family debt must be subtracted from this to obtain net wealth.

For our discussion here we use this straightforward definition of net wealth, omitting social security and defined benefit pension plans. Furthermore, we avoid for the moment the complex debates over the measurement and purpose of wealth. We assume that, all other things being equal, net wealth increases with age and peaks in the age group just prior to retirement.[2] This assumption requires no behavioral hypothesis; it simply reflects what is observed in actual data.

FINDINGS

Using these simplifying tenets, we examine changes in the growth in net wealth and the potential effects of these changes on various age groups. Four conclusions emerge from our analysis:

☐ The growth in net wealth per household experienced a dramatic slowdown during the 1970s and was virtually stagnant between 1972 and 1983. Unlike income, however, the slower growth in net wealth per household began in the 1960s rather than the 1970s.
☐ As is the case with income, the slowdown in growth of net wealth during the 1970s affected young households the most. Between 1973

and 1986, the net wealth of families with heads ages 25–34 declined from 53 percent of the average net wealth for all families to 28 percent. A little less than half of this decline occurred since 1979. In contrast, the relative net wealth standings of older households increased steadily since the late 1970s. Between 1977 and 1986, the net wealth of families with heads over 65 increased from 115 percent of the average net wealth for all families to 165 percent.

□ If we look at cohorts, it becomes clear that members of the baby boom generation have fared far less well than members of their parents' cohort or the cohort of their older siblings. Members of the baby boom generation did start their working lives with a higher level of net wealth than their parents' generation. But because the *growth* in their net wealth is unlikely to match that of their parents, they will probably approach retirement in a relatively less comfortable net wealth position.[3]

□ Young family heads with more than a high school education have higher net wealth but also significantly higher debts than young family heads with a high school education or less. However, as they age, home equity diminishes significantly as an important factor in the net wealth of better educated families, while it remains the single most important factor among lesser educated ones. This means that the future economic stability of families with less education is much more dependent upon a strong housing market.

A SLOWDOWN IN THE GROWTH OF NET WEALTH

As we have shown earlier, wage and family income growth slowed considerably after 1973. Was there a similar deterioration in the growth rate of net wealth?

As table 5.1 shows, real net wealth per household in the 1970s grew at an annual rate that was one-sixth as high as the growth rate of the 1950s.[4] Unlike the growth in median family income, however, the growth of net wealth began slowing during the 1960s, well before the economic stagnation of the post-1973 period.[5]

What were the causes of the slower growth in net wealth per household and why did it start before the decline in income? There have been two common responses to this question in recent years. One is that foreign net wealth replaced domestic net wealth because of the significant shift in the world's economic power first toward oil-producing nations and then toward Japan. This explanation is

Table 5.1 THE SLOWDOWN IN NET WEALTH GROWTH

	Average annual percent growth[a]			
	Real income measures		Real net wealth measures	
	Per capita income	Median family incomes	Per capita net wealth	Per household net wealth
1950s (1949–58)	+2.4	+3.6	+3.0	+2.7
1960s (1958–69)	+3.5	+3.9	+1.9	+1.3
1970s (1972–83)	+1.8	−.0[b]	+1.6	+.4

Source: Wealth data are derived from Wolff and Marley (1989), Table 2; the concept used here is referred to as W-1, defined as the cash surrender value of tangible and financial assets, including home equity, less liabilities. Per capita income data are from the Survey of Current Business (July 1982 and July 1986); family income data are from U.S. Bureau of the Census P-60 reports, various years.
a. All basic figures adjusted to constant 1987 dollars using the PCE deflator.
b. The average rate of change was negative but less than .05%.

plausible in the post-1973 period. It cannot, however, explain the significant growth decline in the 1960s, which occurred prior to the 1973 and 1979 oil price increases and prior to the rapid rise in the U.S. trade and investment imbalances of the 1980s.

A second and more subtle explanation for the decline in the growth of U.S. net wealth is that the number of households was growing more rapidly than aggregate net wealth. Related to this is the argument that the age distribution of household heads shifted dramatically toward younger household heads who typically have a lower than average net wealth. Let us deal with each of these arguments in turn.

It is true that the rate of household formation in the United States has increased somewhat in recent decades relative to the 1950s. But this rate has not outpaced the growth in aggregate net wealth. Between 1949 and 1958, for example, the number of new households grew by 20 percent and aggregate net wealth grew by 49 percent. But between 1958 and 1969, the number of households in the U.S. grew by 22 percent while aggregate net wealth grew by 40 percent. Similarly, between 1972 and 1983, the growth rates were 26 percent for households and 31 percent for aggregate net wealth. Thus, although the acceleration of household formation certainly played a role, it seems clear that the slowdown in the growth of aggregate net wealth was the more significant factor in depressing the growth rates in per household net wealth.

What about the shift in the age distribution of household heads?

There is no doubt that in the 1970s the percentage of households headed by young persons increased significantly and probably exerted a downward influence on per household net wealth. In 1970, 18.5 percent of households were headed by a person between the ages of 25 and 34; by 1980 this figure had increased to 22.9 percent.[6] But no such similar shift occurred in the 1960s when the slowdown in the growth of net wealth began. In 1960, 18.4 percent of households were headed by a person between the ages of 25 and 34, almost exactly the same as in 1970.

Given that neither foreign displacement of domestic wealth nor household demographics seem to adequately explain the two-decade decline in the growth of household wealth, what other factors were at work? The growth of net wealth can be affected by many economic factors, including savings behavior, interest rates, the price of real estate, and the value of stocks. If members of a society have a strong propensity to save rather than consume, net wealth will rise. If interest rates are high relative to prices, creditor households will experience gains in net wealth while debtor households will lose ground. And if growth in real estate or equities is strong, owners of those assets will benefit. Government tax policy also plays a role, not only in providing incentives for certain kinds of investment,[7] but also in establishing tax levels that can change the ability of individuals and families to save and invest. Did any of these factors affect the growth in household wealth during the 1960s and 1970s?

When we look at the 1970s, we find several economic events that are consistent with the dramatic slowdown in the growth of net wealth in that decade. The oil price increases in 1973 and 1979, the entrance of the baby boom generation and women into the labor force, and the slowdown in worker productivity all exerted a downward influence on wage and income growth. This in turn created less saving and more debt. The decade also started with a mild economic recession and experienced a more severe one during 1974 and 1975. Tax burdens rose dramatically. The total tax burden on a median income family was nearly 70 percent higher at the end of the decade than at the start of it.[8] In general, the 1970s were tough times, and it is not surprising that this fact was reflected in the growth rate of per household wealth.

It is less clear why wealth accumulation slowed in the 1960s. There were no recessions in the 1960s, incomes were rising dramatically (see table 5.1), and interest rates were low relative to today. Housing prices were growing steadily. And although tax burdens were rising, the increase for a median income family amounted to only about 2 percent of disposable income.[9] Furthermore, savings rates were quite high in the 1960s. While real savings per household was virtually constant throughout the 1950s, during the 1960s real savings per household grew by about 7.5 percent per year.[10]

If the value of real assets was rising, income growth was at historical highs, and savings rates were increasing dramatically, why didn't the growth in net wealth continue to rise as rapidly during the 1960s as the 1950s? There are two possible answers: a stagnation in equity markets and a growth in personal debt that failed to slow from the heady increases of the 1950s.

Although the equity market stagnation did not affect everyone, the change from the 1950s was dramatic. Between 1953 and 1962, for example, the average real growth rate in the total Dow Jones Index was more than 8 percent per year. Between 1962 and 1969, the index grew at a much slower average of 1.8 percent per year. Then, between 1969 and 1973, the index *declined* rapidly at a rate of more than 5 percent per year. Over the whole period from 1962 to 1973, the real value of the index declined by 1 percent per year on average.[11] Thus, the value of stocks for many households declined over the course of the decade, which certainly served to mitigate the overall growth of net wealth.

An equally important trend was the growth in personal debt per household. Household debt as a proportion of wealth has been steadily increasing in the United States since the early 1900s.[12] But the rate of increase accelerated after the 1950s. Our calculations in table 5.2 show that during the 1960s, while the growth in *gross* wealth per household was falling dramatically, the growth in debt per household continued unabated. During the 1950s, for example, personal

Table 5.2 THE GROWTH OF DEBT IN COMPARISON TO WEALTH

Time Period	Gross wealth	Debt	Net wealth	Radio of debt growth to gross wealth growth
	(1987 dollars per household per year)			
1949–58	+3,284	+929	+2,355	.28
1958–69	+2,479	+1,019	+1,396	.41
1972–83	+915	+414	+501	.45

Source: Wealth data are derived from Wolff and Marley (1989), Table 2. The concept of gross wealth used here is referred to as W-1, defined as the cash surrender value of tangible and financial assets, including home equity. Individual liability data are from the Flow of Funds Statements of the Federal Reserve Board (August 1983 and September 1986).

liabilities per household increased by 28 cents per year for every dollar growth in gross wealth, which refers to total assets before subtracting debt. This meant that the dollar increase in *net* wealth per household was more than twice as high as the dollar increase in liabilities. During the 1960s, however, households did not adjust to the decline in the growth of gross wealth. While the annual increase in per household gross wealth declined from $3,284 to $2,479, the annual increase in per household liabilities rose somewhat, from $929 to $1,019 (in 1987 dollars). In other words, during the 1960s personal liabilities per household increased by 41 cents per year for every dollar increase in gross wealth. This, of course, led to the significant decline in the growth of per household *net* wealth.

The effect of the aforementioned economic problems of the 1970s on the growth of wealth was even more dramatic. The annual per household growth in gross wealth dropped from $2,479 over the decade of the 1960s to $915 between 1972 and 1983. Households apparently attempted to adjust by reducing the rate at which they accumulated debt. The annual growth rate of per household personal liabilities dropped from $1,019 during the 1960s to $414 in the 1970s. But because the rate of gross wealth accumulation was dropping even faster, net wealth growth per household dropped by almost two-thirds.

The picture that emerges from examining three decades of net wealth growth is a complicated one. Although it is clear from the 1970s data that downward shifts in the economy dramatically affect the growth in net wealth, the experience of the 1960s shows that net wealth growth can slow even if general economic growth is robust.

Furthermore, the components of net wealth growth are so varied that a slowdown in the overall growth rate does not imply that all households or families having some net wealth are affected similarly. In the next sections, we examine how net wealth is distributed across families and how different age groups and cohorts can have very different experiences in net wealth growth depending on when in their life cycle various financial changes occur.

THE FORTUNATE GENERATION: THE 1929–1938 COHORT

The distribution of wealth is far less equal across U.S. families than the distribution of income. As table 5.3 shows, the 20 percent of families who receive the most income typically receive 40 to 43

Table 5.3 COMPARISONS OF THE DISTRIBUTION OF NET WEALTH AND INCOME BY FAMILY QUINTILES FOR SELECTED YEARS

	Percent of total held by families in					
Year	Lowest quintile	2nd	3rd	4th	Highest quintile	Highest 5 percent
Net wealth						
1962	−.3	1.2	5.3	12.9	80.9	54.6
1973	<.1>[a]		3.5	11.7	84.7	57.5
1979	−.2	2.6	8.2	18.4	70.9	36.8[b]
1983	−.2	1.8	5.9	13.6	78.8	53.3
Cash income						
1962	5.0	12.1	17.6	24.0	41.3	15.7
1973	5.5	11.9	17.5	24.0	41.1	15.5
1979	5.2	11.6	17.5	24.1	41.7	15.8
1983	4.7	11.0	17.0	24.4	42.9	16.0

Source: *For net wealth.* 1962: 1962 Survey of the Financial Characteristics of Consumers, Wolff and Marley (1989); 1973: merged Census and income tax return data, Greenwood (1987); 1979: 1979 Income Survey Development Program file, Radner and Vaughn (1984); 1983: 1983 Survey of Consumer Finances, Wolff and Marley (1989). *For income.* "Money Income of Families and Persons in the United States: 1984." U.S. Bureau of the Census, P-60 Series, No. 148, Table 12.
a. Greenwood (1987) provides estimates only for the lowest 40 percent of the wealth distribution.
b. The 1979 study by Radner and Vaughn shows a more equal distribution of wealth than other studies. We think this is an artifact of the data and not a real shift. Nevertheless, their figures confirm that wealth is more concentrated than income.

percent of all income, while the 20 percent of families who hold the most wealth typically hold between 70 and 80 percent of all wealth. This contrast is even sharper at the very top of the distributions. In 1983, for example, the 5 percent of families with the highest income received about 16 percent of all income, the 5 percent of families with the most wealth held more than 50 percent of all net wealth.

Although there is some relationship between high income and high wealth, several researchers have recently reported that variation in income explains less than 20 percent of the variation in wealth.[13] Some individuals at the same income level clearly save more than others or invest more fortuitously, and this probably explains why income variations do not explain a large percentage of wealth holdings when all other family factors are the same.

Wealth is accumulated in several ways including savings, the appreciation of assets, and inheritances. But except for inheritances, most of these processes require the passage of time. Thus the older a person is, the more likely he or she is to have larger wealth holdings, all other factors being equal.[14] Age is therefore a critical element in the distribution of wealth across the population.

One means of examining the relative economic well-being of a generation is to examine the distribution of wealth holdings across age groups. Several important studies have generated such distributions.[15] But in almost every case, the studies used somewhat different measurement concepts of net wealth.

In general, all used the same components of gross wealth and debt, including home value less mortgages plus or minus other financial holdings and obligations, but excluding social security and defined-benefit pension wealth. The most common differences are in the sample design and the precise questions in the base surveys, but the analysts have introduced further differences. Some analysts have discarded observations they regard as inconsistent, some have adjusted survey totals to match national income accounts data, and one group has used medians instead of means, which can be substantially different because of the skewed distribution of wealth.

Although we cannot adjust for all the variance in measurement techniques, two approaches can help us interpret what these studies show about the distribution of assets over time. The first borrows from a technique recently employed by Greenwood and Wolff (1988). We calculate the ratios of the median or mean assets of families with heads in each age group to the median or mean assets of all families for each study. In this way, we can partially control for editing and measurement differences by assuming that the edits had a roughly proportional impact on each age group. The ratios resulting from this calculation are shown in table 5.4. As can be seen from the 1983 results in this table, this ratio method roughly standardizes for variant editing and imputation techniques. The ratios for each of two different 1983 studies are quite close to each other with only a single (unexplainable) exception, the ratio for families headed by persons ages 45–54.

The second method of controlling for differences is simply to compare changes over time only within studies, that is to measure changes between time periods for which net wealth has been calculated in exactly the same manner. Fortunately, there are three such groupings embedded in table 5.4 and these groupings provide us with measures of change for approximately each ten years since 1953. Katona (1963) can be used to measure changes from 1953 to 1962. Greenwood and Wolff (1988) can be used to measure changes from 1962 to 1973 to

Table 5.4 THE RELATIVE DISTRIBUTION OF FAMILY WEALTH, 1953–1983
(As a ratio of the age group average for all families)

| | (As a ratio of the age group average to the average for all families) | | | | | | | |
	1953	1962a	1962b	1973	1977	1979	1983a	1983b
Familes headed by a person age								
<25	.07	.05	.12	.25	.17	.14	.10	.10
25–34	.51	.38	.34	.59	.46	.39	.33	.35
35–44	1.09	1.28	.77	.91	1.09	1.04	.83	.87
45–54	2.01	2.11	1.04	1.07	1.46	1.27	1.57	1.20
55–64	2.10	2.12	1.58	1.20	1.51	1.69	1.70	1.75
65+	2.05	1.70	1.52	1.59	1.15	1.27	1.52	1.42
All families	1.00	1.00	1.00	1.00	1.00	1.00	1.00	1.00

Source: 1953 and 1962a: 1953 Survey of Consumer Finances and 1962 Survey of the Financial Characteristics of Consumers, Katona et al. (1963); 1962b: 1962 SFCC, Greenwood and Wolff (1988); 1973: merged census and income tax return data, Greenwood and Wolff (1988); 1977: 1977 Survey of Consumer Finances, Weicher and Wachter (1986); 1979: 1979 Income Survey Development Program file, Radner and Vaughn (1984); 1983a and 1983b: 1983 Survey of Consumer Finances, Greenwood and Wolff (1988), and Weicher and Wachter (1986), respectively.
Note: The figures for 1953 and 1962a are medians. All others are means.

1983.[16] Further analysis for a briefer period from 1977 to 1983 can be derived from Weicher and Wachter (1986). The results of these groupings are shown in table 5.5.

What story does this tell about shifting distributions of net wealth since 1953? A careful examination of the data in tables 5.4 and 5.5, coupled with liberal use of other economic and financial data, yields the following story.

The story begins with the fact that during the 1950s, the relative net wealth status of the youngest families deteriorated when compared to the wealth status of similar age groups in earlier periods. The real net wealth of families headed by a person age 25 to 34, for example, experienced a significant decline between 1953 and 1962 relative to the net wealth of an average family, dropping from 51 percent to 38 percent (table 5.4). These families also experienced an absolute decline of 11 percent in their real net wealth (table 5.5). During this same period, however, the absolute net wealth positions of families headed by a person aged 65 or more also deteriorated somewhat, while the situation for families headed by persons above 35 but below 65 improved dramatically.

During the 1960s the relative and absolute net wealth of young families improved dramatically. The Greenwood and Wolff figures show that for families headed by a 25- to 34-year-old, the ratio of net wealth to the average net wealth for all families rose from 34 percent to 59 percent between 1962 and 1973.[17] Furthermore, the absolute net wealth for these families rose by more than 100 percent during this period. In contrast, older families in this period main-

Table 5.5 GROWTH RATES IN REAL NET WEALTH BY AGE GROUP, 1953–1983
(percent)

	Katona (1963)	Greenwood-Wolff (1988)		Weicher-Wachter (1986)
	1953–1962	1962–1973	1973–1983	1977–1983
Families headed by persons age				
<25	− 13.4	+ 152.1	− 60.6	− 33.4
25–34	− 11.3	+ 106.4	− 42.3	− 19.2
35–44	+ 39.2	+ 39.8	− 6.1	− 11.6
45–54	+ 24.5	+ 22.1	+ 51.9	− 6.3
55–64	+ 20.5	− 10.3	+ 46.9	+ 30.0
65 +	− 1.0	+ 23.6	− 1.0	+ 34.9
All families	+ 19.2	+ 17.9	+ 3.5	+ 7.8

tained approximately the same level of relative net wealth and experienced smaller, but still significant, increases in their absolute net wealth.[18]

The increase in the net wealth status of younger families reversed itself sometime between 1973 and 1977 and the decline continued after 1977, both in absolute and relative terms. For families headed by a person aged 25–34, the ratio of their net wealth to average net wealth declined from 59 percent in 1973 to 33 percent in 1983.[19] The real value of net wealth for this group declined by 42 percent in this period, with about 45 percent of the decline occurring after 1977. Significant losses were also absorbed by families with heads less than 25 and those between 35 and 44. During this same period, families with heads between 45 and 65 experienced strong increases in the real value of their net wealth, rising by rates close to or exceeding 50 percent. Families headed by a person age 65 or more lost a little ground during the 1970s but experienced strong gains after 1977.

These figures imply that younger families fared best with respect to net wealth accumulation before 1973 and their relative and absolute net wealth holdings have declined since then. The figures in tables 5.4 and 5.5 answer the question "How well are younger families today doing relative to families of similar age in previous decades?" We believe this is an important question to ask because it tells us something about the historical status of families in each age group. This historical context helps us understand how each new generation is doing with respect to previous ones at the same age. This, in turn, allows us to determine whether the society as a whole is moving forward or slipping back with respect to family economic progress.

Some critics of this approach have argued that this is the wrong question, that the real issue for most individual families is whether they continue to improve their own economic status from year-to-year, even if the improvement is somewhat less than that of previous generations. We think both questions are important, and we now attempt to answer the second question as well. While we cannot look at the progress of individual families using these data, we can use the studies to examine the progress of cohorts of families over some periods of their life cycle.

In order to do this, we borrow a technique from Lansing and Sonquist (1969).[20] We assume that there are several cohorts of family heads represented in the data from the various studies we have assembled here. For example, the cohort of 1919–1928 would have been 25–34 in 1953, (roughly) 35–44 in 1962, 45–54 in 1973, and so on. Taking the midpoint of our age groups (e.g. the midpoint of persons ages 25–34 is 30), we can follow each cohort as it moves from its twenties to its thirties, thirties to forties, etc., again by pairing studies that provide consistent measures of net wealth.[21]

The results of these calculations are shown in table 5.6. In general, these figures tell an interesting story about baby boomers, their parents, and their older siblings, a story that is consistent with the one told in tables 5.4 and 5.5. Members of the baby boom generation, the cohort of 1949–1958, experienced positive growth in their real net wealth during their twenties, but at a far lower rate than the wealth of their parents' or even their older siblings' or cousins' generation. The cohort that best approximates the parents of baby boomers (1929–1938) experienced a 524 percent increase in their real net wealth during their twenties, while baby boomers experienced an increase of only 34 percent.

Furthermore, the cohort that best approximates the older brothers and sisters of baby boomers (1939–1948) experienced a 485 percent increase during their twenties, a growth not significantly different from that of the cohort of 1929–1938.

The figures in table 5.6 show that the most fortunate cohort consists of those persons who were born between 1929 and 1938, the group that we have loosely identified as the parents of baby boomers. In the early phases of their lives, these cohort members have outperformed succeeding and preceding cohorts, sometimes by substantial margins.

The figures in tables 5.6, coupled with those in table 5.5, also show that today's elderly (age 65 and above) have been the recipients of some good fortune over the past 30 years, but have not experienced

Table 5.6 ANALYSIS OF THE GROWTH IN REAL NET WEALTH BY SELECTED AGE COHORT, 1953–1983

| | Percent Growth between Ages | | | |
	20–30	30–40	40–50	50–60
Cohort Birth Years				
1909–1918	n/a	n/a	+130	+37
1919–1928	n/a	+196	+65	+65
1929–1938	+524	+219	+79	n/a
1939–1948	+485	+45	n/a	n/a
1949–1958	+34	n/a	n/a	n/a

n/a = Not available from sources cited in table 5.4.

increases in net wealth universally superior to other age groups. While the members of the cohort of 1919–1928 have increased their net wealth significantly since 1953, the members of the cohort of 1909–1918 have experienced relatively modest increases. Table 5.5 also shows that the elderly as a group experienced only a modest net gain between 1953 and 1973, and actually experienced a slight decline in the 1950s. The biggest gain for this age group appears to have come only recently, from 1977–1983, but this brief period is the only one in which they outperformed other age groups in terms of real growth in net wealth.

Why should the cohort of 1929–1938 have outperformed other cohorts at similar stages of their lives? One factor may be their attitudes toward consumption and savings that resulted from living through the Great Depression and World War II as children. But to a large extent this was a matter of being in the right place at the right time. The members of this cohort moved through their twenties roughly in the 1950s and through their thirties in the 1960s, periods of strong economic growth for the U.S. economy—growth that was very evident in family incomes. By the time the post-1973 U.S. economic difficulties began, individuals in this cohort had already accumulated significant wealth holdings, including homes whose values were rising faster than general prices, and thus had some insulation from income stagnation and inflation. To understand how timing worked in favor of this cohort, it is useful to think about the components of wealth among the various age groups.

The most significant component of a given family's wealth is equity in the family home. Between 1953 and 1983, the ratio of home equity to net wealth for the average family remained between 45 and 55 percent.[22] While home equity typically remains the single largest element, its importance as a component of net wealth decreases with the age of the family head. As families begin to accumulate wealth they diversify their asset portfolios, and the value of cash savings, bonds, and stocks becomes a more important component of net wealth. As illustrated in table 5.7, for young families in 1983 the value of financial assets was less than a quarter of the value of home equity, whereas for families with heads ages 55–64, the value of financial assets was almost 80 percent of the value of home equity.

This makes sense for a number of reasons. Young families typically save funds to buy a house and thus their early financial assets are converted into home equity in the form of down payments. Having purchased a home, families then begin to save and invest for other purposes, including retirement. As they approach or reach retirement

Table 5.7 FAMILIES HOLDING VARIOUS KINDS OF ASSETS IN 1983

Age of Family Head	Percent owning homes	Mean home equity (1987 dollars)	Mean financial assets (1987 dollars)	Percent owning					
				Money market accounts	CDs	IRAs	Stocks	Bonds
<25	20% ⎤	36,155	3,037 ⎤	8	9	9	13	1
25–34	46% ⎦	59,769	9,141 ⎦	16	16	19	22	3
35–44	66%	74,004	16,546	12	18	25	22	3
45–54	75%	84,462	26,413	18	30	33	25	5
55–64	73%	66,889	63,080	18	37	8	21	4
65+	70%		N/A					

Source: Avery et al. (1984a) and tabulations by the authors from the 1983 Survey of Consumer Finances.
n/a = not available

age, some individuals pull some or all of the equity from their homes and convert it to financial assets, thus increasing the relative importance of financial holdings in older age groups.

Table 5.7 also shows how an increasing proportion of older households own certain kinds of assets that are sensitive to interest rates or changes in stock values. In the 55–64 age group, more than twice as many families own money market accounts, certificates of deposit (CDs), IRA accounts, stocks, and bonds as is the case for younger families.

How did these demographic ownership rates work in favor of the cohort of 1929–1938 during their working years? Again we must consider the macroeconomic environment in which this cohort matured. Table 5.8 shows some proxy measures of growth for key assets in the portfolios of many households. The growth in real median new home values is used as a proxy for the appreciation in the value of homes, though in fact it probably understates the appreciation that actually occurs.[23] The real growth in the Dow Jones total (not just the industrial) index is used to approximate the growth in the value of equities.[24] The interest rate on three-year Treasury notes is used to approximate the return on interest-bearing investments such as bonds, savings accounts, certificates of deposit, and money market accounts.

The figures show why the cohort of 1929–1938 benefited from timing. Individuals in this cohort were just entering the labor force in the early 1950s and were beginning to buy homes. In the 1950s the real returns to home ownership were substantial, by our calculation averaging 3.3 percent per year between 1953 and 1962. Rates

Table 5.8 AVERAGE ANNUAL REAL RATES OF RETURN ON SELECTED INVESTMENTS, 1953–1983
(percent)

Period	New home[a]	Stocks[b]	3-Year treasury notes
1953–62	3.3	8.5	1.4
1962–73	4.2	− 1.0	1.9
1962–69	5.7	1.8	2.2
1969–73	1.2	− 5.3	1.8
1973–83	1.0	− 2.2	1.8
1973–77	2.9	− 5.4	− .2
1977–83	− .2	-0-	3.0

Note: All figures are deflated by the PCE deflator.
a. As measured by the increase in the median sales price of a new home.
b. As measured by the growth in the total Dow Jones Index.

of return on stocks were much higher than those on housing and rates of return on interest-bearing securities were low but still positive. These trends are not as important as the trends in returns to home ownership, however. Stocks affected only a few members of this cohort at that time and the return on interest-bearing securities served basically to maintain the value of their savings.

In the 1960s, as the members of the 1929–1938 cohort reached their thirties, almost two-thirds owned their own homes.[25] During this period, the appreciation on homes increased even more than in the 1950s, although the stock market appears to have been a poor investment, particularly in the last two years of the decade. Interest-bearing investments continued to provide secure and relatively high real rates of return, according to our calculations. This harmonized nicely with the fortunes of the 1929–1938 cohort. With their home purchases behind them and with fixed rate mortgages and rising real incomes, this generation was poised to maximize the effects of both the appreciation of their homes and the relatively high returns from interest-bearing investments.[26] In fact, per capita and per worker personal savings rose dramatically in the 1960s, while the growth in consumption continued its pace of the 1950s. Between 1962 and 1973, real per worker savings increased by almost 80 percent while real per worker consumption rose by 25 percent.[27] In some senses, during the 1960s the cohort of 1929–1938 was able to "have it all," increasing its consumption while at the same time saving more and experiencing strong increases in home equity.

As the 1970s began, the members of this cohort further benefited from rapid, and by now compounding, increases in their home equity as other forms of investment faltered. But the savings they had accumulated during the 1960s subsequently helped them weather the difficult period during the late 1970s when home prices stagnated. The relatively high returns to interest-sensitive investments in the period from 1977 to 1983 benefited the members of the 1929–1938 cohort, who had relatively more liquid assets than younger cohorts. The high real interest rates of this period probably also helped the cohorts of 1909–1918 and 1919–1928, and may explain why the elderly as a group made their greatest gains in net wealth in 30 years during this period (see tables 5.4 and 5.5).

Although it certainly gained the most, the cohort of 1929–1938 was not the only one that benefited from the strong economy of the 1950s and 1960s. The cohort of 1939–1948, whom we have called the older siblings of the baby boomers, were by and large passing through their twenties during the 1960s. Incomes were growing rapidly, housing appreciation was strong, and interest rates were relatively stable. Members of this cohort were able to purchase their first home and, like the members of the cohort immediately preceding them, watched the equity grow as their incomes outpaced the fixed-rate mortgages that dominated housing financial markets at the time. Because housing appreciation remained strong in the early 1970s, this group was able to cushion the impact of stagnant incomes. And by the time interest rates shot up at the end of the decade, this 1939–1948 cohort had sufficient savings to further enhance their net wealth position.

THE EFFECTS OF NET WEALTH SHIFTS ON BABY BOOMERS

Members of the baby boom generation did not fare nearly as well as their parents' generation during the post-1973 economic slump. Most were just beginning their working careers in 1973 when the first OPEC oil price increase took effect and the general slowdown in productivity began. Unlike their parents and their older siblings, many had not yet purchased a home by the time the second OPEC increase took effect and the Federal Reserve Bank tightened monetary policy to increase interest rates in 1979. With economic and de-mographic trends dampening their wage growth, and central bank policies pushing mortgage interest rates up, many members of the baby boom confronted a financial squeeze. First, they were too young to have sufficient financial resources to take advantage of the high real interest rates. Second, their wage growth was sufficiently weak to prevent them from accumulating financial wealth. Finally, rising mortgage interest rates combined with rising real estate values to create barriers to their entrance into the housing market.

How badly did the net wealth of this generation suffer as a result of these converging and generally negative events? Some indication is given in tables 5.4, 5.5, and 5.6. The net wealth holdings of the 25–34 age group relative to that of all families declined during the 1970s (table 5.4). Their absolute net wealth declined relative to similarly aged people of prior generations (table 5.5). The cohort of 1949–1958 did experience positive growth in its real net wealth as it moved from its twenties into its thirties (table 5.6). But this growth was significantly lower than the 500 percent growth experienced by baby boomers' parents and older siblings at similar ages, amounting to an increase of only one-third in the baby boomers' real net wealth holdings.

We can look at net wealth in a somewhat different way by examining the ratios of mean net wealth to mean annual income. This ratio gives an indication of how much of a financial cushion a family has against financial misfortune.[28] In general, the younger a person is, the smaller the ratio. In fact, to the extent that one of the major purposes of net wealth is to ensure comfortable retirement, this ratio should peak during an individual's retirement years.

The expected relationships support this hypothesis (table 5.9).[29] Between 1962 and 1983, in each of the three years for which we present data, the ratio of net wealth to income increased steadily as the age of the family head rose.[30] Furthermore, for families with heads over 65, the "normal" retirement age, the ratio peaked. These families had net wealth that was eight to ten times higher than their annual income.

The members of the baby boom generation in 1983 had a net wealth ratio that was slightly lower than that experienced by their parents' generation at a similar age in 1962 (table 5.9). In 1983, families headed by a person age 25–34 had net wealth that was about 1.6 times more than annual income. Families of similar age in 1962 had a net wealth to income ratio of about 1.7. In 1973, however, the ratio for this age group was considerably higher, at about 2.3.

The conclusion to be drawn from these ratios is somewhat ambiguous. Real incomes for families with a head ages 25–34 were actually 15 percent lower in 1983 than in 1973. Thus, the decline in the ratio may be masking a more serious decline in economic well-being for persons in this age group because real income was falling faster than real net wealth over the decade of the 1970s. But it is

Table 5.9 RATIOS OF NET WEALTH TO INCOME, 1962–1983
(Mean net wealth to mean income)

Families headed by a person age	1962	1973	1983
25–34	1.65	2.30	1.56
35–44	3.30	2.93	2.98
45–54	4.20	3.22	5.06
55–64	6.96	4.22	6.24
65 +	10.46	9.36	8.33

Source: Net wealth data derived from Greenwood and Wolff (1988); mean income data from U.S. Bureau of the Census P-60 reports, various years.

also true that compared to the generation age 25–34 in 1962, members of the baby boom generation had real incomes that were 26 percent higher and real net wealth that was 19 percent higher. Thus, if we think of wealth as a means of maintaining current income levels after a financial disruption, the ratios in table 5.9 imply that in 1983 baby boomers were on the whole at least as able to do this as their parents and at a somewhat higher level of income.

In order to better understand the nature of baby boomers' financial status, it is useful to begin by looking at the details of their current net wealth holdings. In table 5.10 we show the components of net wealth for those families headed by a person age 25–34 in 1983. The most striking figure is for home equity, which accounts for 59 percent

Table 5.10 COMPOSITION OF THE NET WEALTH OF BABY BOOMERS IN 1983[a]

	Components of net wealth (1987 dollars)	Percent holding asset or liability
Assets		
Home value	31,571	46
Liquid assets (savings and checking accounts)	2,950	83
IRAs, Keoghs, etc.	417	11
Other financial assets (stocks, bonds, life insurance, etc.)	6,476	39
Illiquid assets (precious metals, jewelry, art, etc.)	1,343	13
Business Assets	7,370	8
Total assets	50,127	
Liabilities[b]		
Home mortgage	11,638	34
Retail debt	1,593	51
Other debt (investment debt, appliance debt, etc.)	2,836	28
Total liabilities	16,067	
Net Wealth	34,060	

Source: Tabulated from the 1983 Survey of Consumer Finances; adjusted to 1987 dollars using the PCE deflator.
a. Baby boomers are represented here by families headed by persons age 25 to 34 in 1983.
b. Assets and liabilities are averaged across the entire age group irrespective of ownership.

of the net wealth of members of this age group. More than four out of five families in this age group have a checking or savings account, but on average it only amounts to 9 percent of their net wealth. Furthermore, the average value of liquid assets in checking and savings accounts was insufficient to cover the average amount of non-housing debt of these families.

Few baby boomers have retirement accounts such as IRAs, and, on average, these are not important components of their net wealth. Stocks, bonds, and life insurance policies with cash values constitute more than 19 percent of net wealth and are held by nearly two out of five families. Such a high proportion of families appears surprising for this age group because it seems unlikely that young persons whose non-housing debt exceeds their liquid assets would invest funds in relatively illiquid instruments. One possible explanation is that these assets were acquired as gifts from older relatives, but this cannot be confirmed from these data.

Business assets appear on average to be an important component of net wealth, but in fact they are concentrated in only about 8 percent of this age group. For those persons who do own such assets, the value is quite high, around $100,000 in 1987 dollars.

It may be useful at this point to discuss the meaning of the average values in table 5.10 (and table 5.11, discussed below). The average baby boom family represented in these tables is a statistical composite and should be viewed in the same light as the "typical American family" that has 2.43 children and .46 dogs. Unlike these statistically average baby boomers, not all young families have some of each asset or debt listed in the tables, and therefore not all of them will be affected by booms or busts in various sectors of the economy. For example, if the bottom fell out of the precious metals' markets (an example of an "illiquid" asset), only 13 percent of all baby boom families at the most would be affected. So while some families might experience a significant decline in net wealth, the vast majority would be untouched by this particular change.[31] Nevertheless, the concept of a statistically average family is a useful analytical tool because it is a means of understanding what happened or will happen to a group of individuals without having to control for every distinguishing characteristic of the members of that group.

The figures in table 5.10 tell us that by far the single most important component of net wealth is the owner-occupied house. Future growth in home equity could by itself allow the members of the baby boom generation to make up some of the growth that was lost during the first decade of their working years. The figures also tell us that a substantial number of baby boomers could benefit from growth in equities markets (i.e., stocks and bonds) and that a very high proportion of baby boomers might benefit from wage growth that would allow them to increase their liquid asset position. Commodity market shifts and entrepreneurial incentives are unlikely to affect very many of them, however.

American families seem to understand the importance of home equity as the cornerstone of wealth. This is reflected in the way young families responded to the enormous changes in housing prices and housing finance after the late 1970s. The story is a familiar one but bears repeating.

Let us begin by seeing how single-earner families were affected by these changes in the housing market.[32] In 1983 it took more than 40 percent of the income of a 30-year-old male to pay the principal and interest on a median-priced home.[33] This contrasts with a figure of roughly 20 percent in 1973 and 15 to 18 percent in the 1950s and 1960s. Even if we account for the fact that in 1983 many young families had two earners and thus family income was higher than the income of young males alone in 1983, the increased burden on families is clear. The percentage of a young family's income necessary to pay the principal and interest on a median-priced home nearly doubled in 30 years, going from 15 to 16 percent in the 1950s, 1960s, and even early 1970s to 28 percent in 1983.[34]

The effects of this increased burden showed in home ownership rates. Between 1973 and 1983, there was about a 4 percentage point decline in the number of households headed by people under 35 who owned their own homes.[35] This meant that approximately one million fewer young householders owned their own homes in 1983 than would have been true a decade earlier. Nevertheless, considering the enormous increase in housing costs relative to income, it is surprising that the decrease in home ownership rates among younger families was not even greater. The modest nature of the decline is an indication of how important families believe owning a home is.[36]

In fact, in 1983 the mean net wealth of all families who owned their homes was more than nine times the net wealth of those who did not.[37] The figures in table 5.10 provide further evidence of the dominance of home ownership in the net wealth equation.

Income is clearly a factor limiting young families in gaining access to the housing market. But the figures we have just presented show that, with some sacrifice, baby boomers were able to overcome the income and financial barriers to buying their own homes, enough so that they were able to maintain home ownership rates roughly at historical levels.

We know that averages across broad groups can sometimes be misleading. In chapter 3 of this book, for example, we showed that macroeconomic changes in recent years had disproportionately affected the wages and incomes of young individuals with a high school education or less, even though some average income figures showed positive results across the entire age group. Has the same impact been observed in the distribution of net wealth among young families?

THE ROLE OF EDUCATION IN NET WEALTH GROWTH

In table 5.11 we repeat the profile of assets and liabilities for baby boomers from table 5.10 but show the differences between those with a high school education or less and those with at least some college education. The table shows that the more educated, even when they are young, have greater net wealth and a stronger and more diversified wealth portfolio than the less educated.

The net wealth of those families headed by a young person with at least some college education was 66 percent higher than that of families headed by a young person with a high school education or less. In general, the more educated families also held more kinds of assets than the less educated. They were twice as likely to have IRA or Keogh accounts and business assets and more than twice as likely to have illiquid assets such as precious metals, jewelry, or art. The value of their liquid assets was more than twice that of the less educated and, while they held more debt for things such as investments, the size of their retail debt was considerably smaller.

The more educated families also tended to have more expensive homes and more mortgage debt, though the net equity in their homes was 27 percent higher than that of less educated families. A critical point shown in table 5.11 is that of home ownership rates: 49 percent of those with a high school education or less owned their homes compared to 44 percent of those with some college education. Although this difference is probably not significant from a statistical perspective, it does show that the tendency to make a home the linchpin of net wealth is at least equally strong among the less educated young as among the more educated.[38]

Furthermore, the importance of home equity appears to be greater

Table 5.11 COMPOSITION OF THE NET WEALTH OF BABY BOOMERS BY EDUCATION STATUS IN 1983
(1987 dollars)

	High school or less		Some college or more	
	Value (1987 dollars)	Percent holding asset or liability	Value (1987 dollars)	Percent holding asset or liability
Assets				
Home value	23,620	49	33,745	44
Liquid assets	1,623	82	3,493	84
IRAs, Keoghs, etc.	222	7	532	13
Other financial assets	3,238	32	7,736	45
Illiquid assets	228	8	2,192	17
Business assets	5,070	5	8,309	9
Total assets	34,001		56,007	
Liabilities				
Home mortgage	8,343	33	12,796	34
Retail debt	2,107	50	815	52
Other debt	705	24	4,411	32
Total liabilities	11,155		18,022	
Net Wealth	22,846		37,985	

Source: Tabulated from the 1983 Survey of Consumer Finances; adjusted to 1987 dollars using the PCE deflator.
a. Baby boomers are represented here by families headed by persons age 25 to 34 in 1983.
b. Assets and liabilities are averaged across the entire age group irrespective of ownership.

among the less educated. Among those families headed by a person with a high school education or less, home equity accounted for more than two-thirds of net wealth. Among those families headed by a person with at least some college education, home equity accounted for about 55 percent of net wealth. Among the less educated, the reliance on home equity seems to remain strong as the family head ages, while it decreases substantially among the more educated. In 1983, for example, among family heads in the 55–64 category, home equity accounted for 64 percent of net wealth among the less educated and only 40 percent among the more educated (table 5.12). This implies that throughout their lives, persons with a high school education or less are dependent primarily upon increasing home values and decreasing mortgage loan balances to sustain the growth in their net wealth. More educated persons begin with a more diversified wealth portfolio and higher income, so they have a greater number of opportunities to realize growth in their net wealth even if there is a slump in the housing market.

To some degree, then, the less educated have all their eggs in one basket when it comes to net wealth growth. If, for example, real house prices collapse in response to a downward shift in housing demand during the 1990s, as some analysts have predicted,[39] these families could experience a serious deterioration in their net wealth positions.

HAS ANYTHING CHANGED SINCE 1983?

Much of the analysis we have done to this point ends with family net wealth data in 1983. This was desirable from our perspective because we wished to analyze trends by cohort and by decade and

Table 5.12 THE IMPORTANCE OF HOME EQUITY IN FAMILY WEALTH IN 1983

Families headed by a person age	Ratio of home equity to total net wealth	
	High school or less	At least some college
25–34	.67	.55
35–44	.77	.35
45–54	.58	.25
55–64	.64	.40
65 +	.50	.38

Source: Authors' tabulations from the 1983 Survey of Consumer Finances.

to examine the decade just after the major economic slowdown that began in 1973.

We now add data from the 1986 Survey of Consumer Finances (SCF), to give us three more years. This is too short a time period to allow clean definitions of cohorts or to detect long-term trends, but examining the data does tell us something about the stability of the relationships detected up to 1983.

In table 5.13, we show selected results from the 1986 SCF and compare them with 1983.[40] The 1986 figures indicate three potentially important results:

□ The relative net wealth position of families headed by persons aged less than 65 deteriorated somewhat between 1983 and 1986, while the relative position of families with a head 65 or more strengthened.

□ Families with heads of all ages experienced a decrease in the ratio

Table 5.13 CHANGE BETWEEN 1983 AND 1986: SELECTED TABULATIONS FROM TWO CONSUMER FINANCE SURVEYS

Tabulations	1983	1986
Ratio of age group average net wealth to average net wealth for all families, by age group		
25–34 years	.33	.28
35–44	.83	.72
45–54	1.57	1.20
55–64	1.70	1.43
65+	1.52	1.65
All families	1.00	1.00
Ratio of net wealth to mean income, by age group		
25–34 years	1.56	1.37
35–44	2.98	2.69
45–54	5.06	3.98
55–64	6.24	5.39
65+	8.33	9.00
Home ownership among young families (ages 25–34) by education level		
High school or less	.49	.41
At least some college	.44	.43

Source: Authors' calculations from the 1983 and 1986 Surveys of Consumer Finances.

of their net wealth to mean income. The decline was sharpest among families with a head less than 65.

□ There was an apparent decrease in home ownership rates among less educated young families between 1983 and 1986. The ownership rates among more educated young families remained roughly the same.

These results imply that younger families have not yet begun to experience significant real growth in their net asset position, and that families headed by less educated younger persons may be experiencing increasing barriers to entering the housing market. If confirmed by further analyses, this would be troublesome news for the future of young families. While the more educated young have the protection of more diverse asset holdings, the less educated rely primarily on housing equity for growth in their net wealth. If increasing numbers of them are excluded from the housing market, their ability to build financial security over a lifetime will be seriously impaired.

Are the results in table 5.13 plausible? We must be cautious about these figures for a number of reasons. First, as noted above, the time period measured is too short to extrapolate to long-term trends with much confidence. Second, the ratios shown in the table could have declined even while real net wealth was rising. If this was the case, some groups simply experienced more improvement than others, but all groups showed some improvement. Because the figures from the 1983 and 1986 surveys have not been standardized with the same care as the existing studies cited earlier, we cannot yet precisely measure the change in absolute levels of real net wealth between 1983 and 1986.

Finally, the net wealth to mean income ratio changes appear to be driven primarily by a dramatic increase in real mean income across all groups between 1983 and 1986. In this period, every age group experienced a growth rate in real income that averaged more than 4 percent per year. This contrasts with average *decreases* in real income between 1973 and 1983 across all groups but the elderly. Thus, the decline in the net wealth to income ratios could actually represent a positive economic development for families.

Confirmation of the trends in net wealth implied by the figures in table 5.13 must await further analyses. At a minimum, the data show that coming out of the 1982–1983 recession, younger families have not experienced any dramatic turnaround in their *relative* net wealth position, be it positive or negative.

SUMMARY

We began this chapter by arguing that an important component of the economic well-being of families is their net wealth. Our analyses show that in the 1980s the well-being of families headed by persons under 35 had deteriorated relative to families of similar age in the 1970s, and that members of the baby boom generation had experienced significantly lower growth in their net wealth than had their parents or older siblings.

It also appears that families headed by persons with a high school education or less are more dependent upon housing equity to build their net wealth, and therefore have fewer opportunities to exploit variable growth rates among assets, than the more educated. Furthermore, recent changes in housing values and financing may present increasing barriers to home ownership for many of those less educated families.

In the next chapters we show what these trends in net wealth, when combined with income trends discussed earlier, imply for the future economic status of the American middle class.

Notes

1. For exact calculations and a full discussion of this issue, see appendix A.

2. This does not commit us to taking sides in the debate over the Modigliani-Brumberg "life cycle model" hypothesis (Modigliani and Brumberg 1954; Modigliani 1966). This hypothesis argues that individuals accumulate wealth principally to finance consumption during their non-working years. With an ideal outcome, this means retired individuals actually dissave and have zero net wealth at the time of their deaths. Our position is simply that empirical studies have shown a profile in which net wealth increases with age.

3. This point is shown both in this chapter and more explicitly in the projections included at the end of chapter 7.

4. We have used proxy years for each of the decades represented in table 5.1 because there were only selected years for which consistent and adjusted aggregate net wealth figures were available. The aggregate net wealth figures that form the basis of the percentages in table 5.1 are derived from Wolff and Marley (1989).

5. This finding is similar to recent results of Greenwood and Wolff (1989), who used somewhat different data and price adjustments.

6. This percentage remained roughly stable during the 1980s. In 1987, 22.9 percent of households were headed by a 25- to 34-year-old.

7. An example of this in the business sector was the Accelerated Cost Recovery System

depreciation schedules, which were implemented in the early 1980s and led to a boom in real estate development and leasing.

8. See Minarik (1985), p. 45, table 7. Total tax burden here is defined as the sum of federal income tax and social security payroll tax rates. Readers should note that all income figures in this report are *pretax*, not post-tax numbers. The pretax figures are the only ones easily available in a consistent series over the periods we are analyzing.

9. Minarik (1985), as above.

10. Savings per household is calculated using household balance sheet data from the Board of Governors of the Federal Reserve System.

11. The Dow Jones Index was chosen because it represents a portfolio of blue chip stocks that is widely considered to be a measure of the health of the equities markets. The decline was not consistent throughout the 1960s since stock values tend to be volatile from year to year. Additionally, some of the broader stock indices such as the Standard and Poor's 500 actually showed modest gains over the 1960s. But the trend over the course of the decade for all measures of stock growth was clearly much lower than that of the 1950s.

12. See Wolff (1989) for a discussion of this.

13. See Greenwood and Wolff (1988), Greenwood (1987), and Radner and Vaughn (1984).

14. Inheritances are popularly thought to be a major source of family wealth but Avery and Elliehausen (1986) report that 93 percent of all families indicate that more than one-half of their assets comes from savings or earnings.

15. Katona et al. (1963), Radner and Vaughn (1984), Avery et al. (1984b), Weicher and Wachter (1986), and Greenwood and Wolff (1988).

16. The raw 1973 data from Greenwood and Wolff (1988) do not appear to be entirely consistent with the 1962 and 1983 data, perhaps because they are partially synthetic. However, at the suggestion of Edward Wolff we have adjusted the basic numbers for all years to the national balance sheet totals. This should minimize inconsistencies over time.

17. Even if we allow that the 1973 data are somewhat inconsistent, the increase in the relative status of young households is independently confirmed by the 1977 data from Weicher and Wachter (1986).

18. There is an unexplained and perhaps spurious decline in both the relative and absolute net wealth of families headed by a 55- to 64-year-old during this period. Again, this may be related to anomolies in the 1973 data.

19. Data from the 1986 Survey of Consumer Finances, shown in a later table, indicate a further decline in this ratio to 28 percent by 1986.

20. Greenwood and Wolff (1989) also employ this approach to cohort analysis. The cohorts they create are five-year rather than the ten-year ones used here. One result of using narrower cohort bands is that some variations are larger and probably spurious.

21. Given that we only have a few data points, we cannot follow a complete life cycle for every age group, but we do have portions of several.

22. Based on Katona (1963) and the authors' tabulations from the 1983 Survey of Consumer Finances.

23. In general, an increase in housing construction or financing costs probably causes adjustments to be made in the type of new home constructed. Thus, in the high cost periods of the late 1970s, we saw a move toward smaller homes with fewer amenities. See Joint Center for Housing Studies (1985).

24. The Dow Jones total index is a broader measure of stock market growth, though it still concentrates on "blue chip" companies in which the average individual investor (as opposed to institutional investors) is most likely to invest.

25. See Katona et al. (1963).

26. As table 5.5 shows, families headed by persons 45–64, which are the families most likely to own their own homes, fared uniformly well with respect to net wealth growth in the 1970s.

27. This contrasts with the more consumption-oriented period from 1953–1962, when real per worker consumption grew by 23 percent while real per worker savings increased by only 8 percent. Saving per household is calculated using household balance sheet data from the Board of Governors of the Federal Reserve System, 1950–1986.

28. Essentially, it shows for what multiple of a year a family's net wealth could sustain the family assuming zero income and complete fungibility of net wealth.

29. In order to ensure the consistency of net wealth calculations, we have limited the figures in table 5.9 to three years represented by the same research study, that of Greenwood and Wolff (1988).

30. Table 5.9 shows a universally lower ratio at each age level above 35 in the 1973 data. This is not because there was a decline in real net wealth but because 1973 represented a business cycle peak and thus a peak for U.S. family incomes.

31. An exception to this is a change in housing prices, which typically has an impact on rents as well as on the value of owner-occupied homes.

32. We assume here that for young persons the economic situation of a single-earner family is represented by the income of a male worker. This assumption reflects the dominant employment patterns among families prior to the mid-1970s.

33. By 1986, this figure had dropped to around 36 percent, due in large part to declining interest rates. However, in 1987 this small decline was offset by rising home prices and the ratio was back up to 40 percent.

34. In 1986 it dropped slightly to 25 percent but by 1987 was back up to 28 percent.

35. See Joint Center for Housing Studies (1985).

36. Apgar et al. (1985) argue that the principal reason for this was that first-time buyers were less sensitive to interest rates than existing home owners because they could not take advantage of real estate price increases until they bought. As a result, first-time buyers in the late 1970s and early 1980s made more sacrifices, such as buying smaller homes, than existing home owners who were trying to "trade up."

37. See Avery et al. (1984b).

38. This tendency seems to be unchanged over time. Calculations by the authors from data provided in Lansing and Sonquist (1969) show that in 1962, 48 percent of families headed by a person with a high school education or less owned their homes compared to 51 percent of families headed by a person with at least some college education.

39. See Mankiw and Weil (1988).

40. Only a few results are shown because we have not subjected the 1986 data to the same degree of validation and editing as the 1983 data.

Chapter Six

LOOKING TOWARD THE FUTURE: MEN'S INDIVIDUAL INCOMES

To this point, we have summarized the evolution of U.S. living standards through the mid-1980s. In the remainder of this book we turn to the future, and ask how today's young workers and their children will fare vis-à-vis earlier generations. We begin this chapter by examining projected incomes for today's young male workers. Specifically, we ask how the future incomes these young men can expect to earn will compare to the incomes of their fathers.

To make the issue concrete, we consider the case of a father who was 25 years old in 1956, the year in which he had a son. By 1986, the father would have been 55 years old and the son would have been 30.[1] We assume that throughout the father's career, the father had the average income of men of his age and education. With this assumption, the father's income over his working years can be approximated by referring to past census reports. Census reports also give an estimate of the son's 1986 income (at age 30) and so the father–son comparison can be completed by projecting the son's income at age 40 (in 1996) and at age 50 (in 2006).

The son's income can be projected in either of two different ways, a difference we can illustrate by example. Consider predicting the average income of 40-year-old, college-educated men in 1996. A direct approach focuses on the average income of 40-year-old, college educated men as that statistic has varied over time. This leads to estimating the following historical relationship:

1) Income $(40, t) = F(X_i, t)$

where: Income $(40, t)$ is the average income of 40-year-old college educated men in year t;

X_i, t is a vector of independent variables in year t including the level of productivity in year (t), the unemployment in year t, the cohort size of men who are 40 in year t, etc.

If we used the direct approach we would begin the income projection by estimating such an equation for the years 1946–1986.[2] We would then make assumptions about the 1996 values of the independent variables (e.g. the level of productivity, the unemployment rate) and use these values with the estimated coefficients to predict the average 1996 incomes of the men in question.

Alternatively, we can focus not on *income levels* but on *income growth* over, say, a decade. Such a model would begin by estimating an equation of the form:

$$2) \quad \frac{\text{Income } (40, t)}{\text{Income } (30, t - 10)} = G(X_i, t)$$

where: Income $(40, t)$ is the average income of 40-year-old college educated men in year t; Income $(30, t - 10)$ is the average income of the same cohort of men 10 years earlier (when they were aged 30); and

X_i, t is, again, a vector of independent variables including the change in productivity growth over the intervening decade between $(t - 10)$ and t, the change in the unemployment rate over the decade, etc.

Here, too, the equation would be estimated over the period 1946–1986. The estimated coefficients would be combined with projections of future productivity growth, etc., to estimate an income growth factor between ages 30 and 40 over the years 1986–1996—say 28 percent. We would then apply this factor to the men's actual income at age 30 (which we observe in 1986) to project their income at age 40 in 1996.

While the second technique appears less direct, we believe the dynamics of labor market adjustment make it the more accurate of the two. Various evidence suggests that when labor markets are in transition, a disproportionate share of the adjustment falls on entry-level workers. In chapter 3, for example, we saw that when manufacturing employment fell in the early 1980s, the earnings of high school educated men, aged 25–34, fell much more sharply than the earnings of older high school men who were partially protected by job seniority (table 3.3).

This concentrated impact on younger workers has implications for the projection of earnings. In 1973, the earnings of high school men, ages 35–44, were 15 percent higher than the earnings of high school men ages 25–34 (table 3.3). By 1986, this gap had opened from 15 percent to 29 percent as the earnings of younger workers declined sharply. The growing earnings gap between younger and older workers suggests that the passage of 10 years' time will not automatically raise the incomes of today's 30-year-olds to the income levels of today's 40-year-olds. Rather, it suggests that today's young workers may face quite different opportunities than similar workers faced a decade ago. Put differently, today's young workers are on their own "income track," just as the 30-year-old workers of a decade ago were on their own income track. Young workers' future incomes will be influenced by macroeconomic forces, but they will not necessarily retrace the income path of workers who entered the labor market in earlier years.

In sum, if we are to estimate what today's 30-year-olds will be earning in 10 years, we should not simply project forward the earnings of today's 40-year-olds. Rather, we should begin with what today's 30-year-olds are actually making and project forward how much those earnings will grow over time.

We estimate earnings growth equations using multivariate regression analysis and attempting to control for productivity changes, unemployment rate, shifts in service and manufacturing jobs, and education. Separate equations are estimated for the passage from age 30 to age 40, and the passage from age 40 to age 50. Within each time period, equations are estimated for men with a high school education or less and men with at least some college.[3] In the estimates, the growth of individual incomes is explained by a set of four variables:

□ The total growth of nonfarm business productivity between years $(t-10)$ and year (t).

□ For workers with at least some college, the change in the unemployment rate between year $(t-10)$ and year (t).

□ For workers who did not go beyond high school, the change in the availability of manufacturing jobs between year $(t-10)$ and year (t).[4]

□ Education. In the regression based on men with a high school education or less, this $(0,1)$ variable is set to 1 when the observation refers to men who have not finished high school. In the regression based on men with at least one year of college, this $(0,1)$ variable is set to one when the observation refers to men with less than four years of college.[5]

Moving to projections of future earnings requires assuming future values for these independent variables. We assume:

☐ Because of slow labor force growth, the unemployment rate falls to 5 percent and remains at that level.

☐ The economy closes its trade deficit by 1992. This growth in demand, coupled with a projected 3 percent per year growth in manufacturing productivity would raise 1992 manufacturing employment to about its 1979 level.

☐ While productivity growth is central to our story, any prediction is hedged with enormous uncertainty. For this reason, we make two earnings projections. The first is based on productivity growth of 1.25 percent per year, the actual rate of productivity growth between 1980 and 1988. The second projection is based on productivity growth of 1.9 percent per year which approximates long run historical trends.[6]

Estimates of projected earnings are summarized in figures 6.1 and 6.2.

Figure 6.1 displays the father-son comparison for a father and son both of whom have exactly four years of college. The comparison is reasonably optimistic. Despite the post-1973 earnings stagnation, the son, aged 30, earned $26,000 in 1986—about $4,000 more than his father had earned at age 30, in 1961. (All figures are in 1987 dollars). At the same time, the father had the advantage of working about half of his subsequent career in the 1960s and early 1970s when productivity was growing rapidly. If the next twenty years of the son's career see productivity growth of 1.25 percent per year (the 1980–

Figure 6.1 FATHER-SON INCOME COMPARISON, COLLEGE GRADUATES

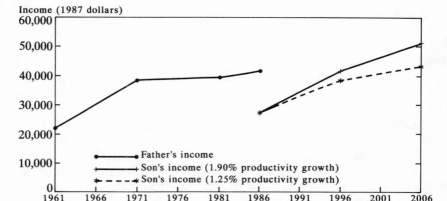

Source: Authors' tabulations from March CPS microdata files.

Figure 6.2 FATHER-SON INCOME COMPARISON, HIGH SCHOOL GRADUATES

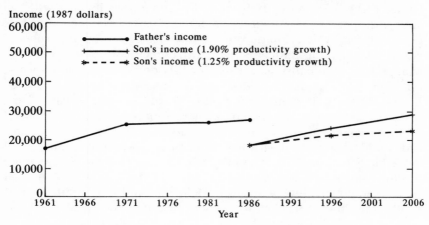

Source: Authors' tabulations from March CPS microdata files.

1988 average rate), we project the son's income at age 50 to reach $43,300. This is $1,700 more than the father earned in 1986, the father's best year. In this slow growth scenario then, the college-educated son outearns his college-educated father, but not by much.

We can see the benefit of high productivity growth by recalculating the father-son comparison with productivity growing annually at 1.9 percent between 1986 and 2006, rather than 1.25 percent. In this case, the college-educated son's income at age 50 reaches $51,200, about $10,000 more than his father's income in his father's best year.

Note that figure 6.1 (and figure 6.2) are projections of a cohort's average income with some cohort members doing better than the average and others doing worse. In the slow growth scenario (1.25 percent productivity growth) the projected income for sons is only slightly better than the actual income of fathers and a son whose earnings are below average (among his peers) has a good chance of not outearning his father. In the faster growth scenario, the gap between an average son's and an average father's incomes is much larger and so a son is likely to outearn his father even if his income is below average among his peers.[7]

Figure 6.2 displays a similar comparison for fathers and sons who have a high school education. Our income projections assume the closing of the trade deficit and the associated increase in labor demand. Despite this improvement, the income projection suggests today's 30-year-old high school graduate will just about equal his father's best years even if productivity grows at 1.9 percent per year. Under the lower productivity path, the son's peak income will be almost 20 percent less than his father's. This pessimistic result reflects the recent deterioration in the incomes of young, high school educated men (table 3.3), which, in turn, reflects continued technical change in manufacturing. Because of this deterioration, a 30-year-old high school graduate had average income only about $1,500 more in 1986 ($18,200)[8] than his then 30-year-old father had earned in 1961. Since the two men's incomes start from roughly similar bases, it would take very rapid productivity growth over the next two decades for the son to outearn his father by a substantial amount.

We have focused on men's individual incomes, but family incomes (for husband-wife families) can be expected to trace generally similar paths at somewhat higher levels. In 1976, husband-wife families with heads ages 25–34[9] had family median income of about $30,500 (in 1987 dollars). Ten years later, this cohort of husband-wife families had a median income of about $39,200.[10] The rate of increase (averaged across all families) looked much more like the earnings increases of college educated men than high school educated men. But much of the gain reflected the fact that over the decade the proportion of families in this group with working wives rose from 52 percent (when they were ages 25–34) to 67 percent (when they were ages 35–44). Today, 66 percent of 25- to 34-year-old husband-wife families already depend on two earners and so there will be less room in the future for family incomes to grow faster than individual incomes by switching to two earners.

It is worth considering the implications of these projections for national life. In chapter 2 we argued that the expansion of the American middle class after World War II depended not so much on lower inequality as on income growth—growth that resulted in greater rates of home ownership, car ownership, vacation travel, and so on.

The large and growing middle class was one example of the upward mobility which has been central to the American dream: the idea that a person can see significant material gains over his or her life and that one's children will do better still. In the years after World War II, rapid economic growth allowed mobility to be both rapid and widespread. People became more secure in their own futures and, in part for this reason, they were more willing to see help go to others. Recall, for example, how the War on Poverty was passed in the middle of the 1960s boom.[11]

How would these things change in a low growth future? As a first approximation, we note that such a future is a projection of the recent past. This means we can get clues to the future by looking around us. The most direct consequence of low economic growth is a slow-down in upward mobility. Upward mobility still exists but not at the mass levels of the 1950s and 1960s. As we saw in chapter 3, for example, it is harder now for high school graduates to earn their way into the middle class than it was 10 years ago. Similarly, young workers at all educational levels are less than certain today that they will outearn their parents.

Lower rates of growth and mobility translate into concerns that spill over into other aspects of national life. For over a decade, the economy has been in a taxpayer's revolt, in which taxes are seen as too high, large deficits are seen as acceptable, and there is generally "no money" for new programs (where new programs range from accelerated space exploration to foreign aid to education). Just as the War on Poverty began in an economic boom, the taxpayer's revolt derives, in part, from continued slow growth: slowly growing in-comes already lag behind consumption aspirations without being further reduced by more taxes. There are undoubtedly many areas where government should be smaller. But when governments are shrinking, it is often the redistributive functions—functions with weak constituencies—that take disproportionate reductions. For ex-ample, when fiscal limits reduce public school expenditures, better-off parents often opt for private schools and lose interest in public school improvement. The nation, as a result, may experience some gains in short-run efficiency but it will be increasingly segmented along economic lines.

By sketching this future, we do not mean to say that economic growth is a cure-all. For the last 20 years, the nation has become increasingly aware of the congestion, pollution, and negative side effects growth often creates. It is important to work to limit these side effects, but it is also important to remember that the costs of growth are often most offensive to persons who have already achieved a comfortable status. For example, in the late 1960s when real wages were growing rapidly, about half of all male college freshmen felt that "being very well off financially" was either an "essential" or "very important" goal in their lives. In the fall of 1973, as growth was beginning to slow, this proportion jumped to 62 percent, and today it stands at 80 percent.[12] During the 1980s, it was common to describe these young people as materialistic, particularly when com-pared to young people of the 1960s. A more plausible explanation is that young people in the 1960s were secure in their economic future (perhaps unrealistically so) while today's young people are more uncertain. This emphasis on making money suggests that economic growth, despite its costs, remains an important goal.

Income, of course, is only one of the components of economic well-being. As discussed in chapter 5, the accumulation of net wealth is a significant, if not equally important, determinant of the economic status of families. Further, while net wealth accumulation is related to income level, many factors that affect the growth of family net wealth are independent of income growth (e.g. the growth of home equity). In the next chapter we look at the future of net wealth for today's young families.

Notes

1. The most recent year of data analyzed for this book is 1986.

2. 1946 is the earliest income data available from the Current Population Survey.

3. In making our projections, we use actual income at age 30 (in 1986) to estimate income at 40 (in 1996) and use estimated income at 40 to estimate income at 50.

4. The availability of manufacturing jobs is defined as the ratio of total manufacturing employment in a given year to the total number of men, ages 25–55, with a high school diploma or less—i.e. the number of jobs divided by an approximation of the number of potential workers.

5. Various descriptions of cohort size were also tested in these equations but they proved generally insignificant. This suggests that in these equations, cohort size has its biggest effect on entry-level income—i.e. a man's income at age 30—and has relatively less effect on subsequent income growth.

6. Productivity growth averaged over 3 percent per year between 1946 and 1973 but this was an exceptionally high figure by historical standards.

7. Note also that the intergenerational mobility embodied in either of these scenarios is far less than the mobility that occurred in the 1950s and 1960s. In those years, a son could be confident in his early thirties that he would outearn his father. Even in the optimistic scenario, a son will be in his early forties before he can be confident he will outearn his father.

8. This figure is somewhat below the figures in table 3.3. Because the estimations in this chapter have to rely on published data for the 1950s and 1960s, the estimates for fathers and sons have to be based on the *median incomes* of all persons rather than the *mean earnings* of persons who worked, the basis for tables 3.2, 3.3, etc. (which were produced from tabulations of the CPS microdata files).

9. We use this age range as an approximation to age 30.

10. Current Population Reports, P-60 series, various issues.

11. Many other factors—the Civil Rights Movement, Lyndon Johnson's political skill—also played important roles in the War on Poverty. But it is unlikely the programs would have been enacted if incomes had been stagnant or declining.

12. See Astin 1989.

Chapter Seven

FAMILY NET WEALTH IN THE FUTURE

Forecasting net wealth growth is as difficult as forecasting wage and income growth, if not more so. The growth of net wealth, as shown above, is a function of individual behavior with respect to savings and consumption, of general economic conditions, and, for most families, a function of the housing subeconomy. Also, for some families net wealth growth may depend upon unpredictable events such as inheritances, insurance settlements, and lotteries.

In chapter 5 we showed how the growth of per household net wealth was strongest during the 1950s and 1960s when economic growth was robust and declined dramatically in the 1970s when the economy was stagnant. But the slower growth in net wealth actually began in the 1960s, despite the fact that income growth in that decade exceeded that of the 1950s. There are many possible explanations for this, but among the more plausible is that the slower net wealth growth in the 1960s was caused by declines in the equities markets, which affects only a small percentage of families but can still have a large impact on average household and family wealth.

We also showed that neither growth nor decline in net wealth is evenly distributed among families at all stages of life. Generations fare differently with respect to net wealth growth depending on where they are in their life cycle when economic booms or busts occur. Some families, for example, fared well even in the post-1973 period, when general economic growth was moribund.

These observations confirm our intuitive notion that many elements affect the future of family net wealth growth. The lack of historical and consistent data on net wealth, however, limits our ability to develop formal forecasting models for predicting the future of net wealth growth.[1] But we can look at some critical elements in the growth of net wealth and see whether they are consistent with the robust growth that occurred among pre-baby boom generations prior to 1973. In this chapter we examine the future of four components of net wealth growth: general economic growth, growth in the housing subeconomy, behavioral changes among families, and inheritances.

GENERAL ECONOMIC GROWTH PROSPECTS

Although growth in net wealth is a function of many events, long-term growth in net wealth cannot occur in the absence of a stable economy. Real growth in wages, for example, permits more savings by families with earnings. Corollary growth in housing markets not only helps families who already own their own homes, but supplies an incentive for non-owners to make short-term sacrifices to obtain their first home. And if general economic growth does not occur too rapidly and is not accompanied by unacceptably high inflation, it will stimulate growth in equities markets.

As discussed earlier, a substantial portion of the gains made by today's older cohorts came because economic circumstances were favorable for these groups in their early and middle years. Wage growth in the 1950s and 1960s was high enough to permit increased savings and increased consumption simultaneously. Although stock appreciation fluctuated, interest rates and home value appreciation were relatively steady, which made for more predictable investment returns for the average American family than we have seen in recent years.

We know that members of the baby boom generation have not been as fortunate as their parents or older siblings with respect to the stability of the growth of the U.S. economy since 1973. Wage growth has been erratic at best, and evidence implies that when wages did grow, they did not grow consistently for all workers. Furthermore, neither the interest nor equity markets has been very predictable since the late 1970s.

As noted in chapter 6, in order to offset the effects of the slow economic growth since 1973 on future wealth, the United States must experience a relatively long period of strong economic growth during the baby boomers' working lives. Ideally, such a period would include rising real incomes (on the order of 2 to 3 percent per year, in contrast to the 1 percent increase of recent years), relatively low but stable real interest rates (to permit baby boomers to enter the housing market and allow them a modest return on interest-sensitive investments), and enough resilience in housing markets to prevent a real estate collapse on a par with the October 1987 stock market crash. Steady growth in equities markets may also help baby boomers, though this is a less important source of net wealth for most families (see table 5.7 above).

Is it reasonable to expect any or all of these factors to occur during the next decade or two before baby boomers begin to retire? We begin our discussion of the future by examining the prospects for economic growth on a scale that would permit young families to increase their net wealth at significantly higher rates than in recent years.

In January 1989 Data Resources Inc. (DRI), one of the nation's best known macroeconomic forecasting firms, published two economic projections for the period between now and the end of the century.[2] These two projections differ in one important respect: one, called the Trend forecast, assumes that the slow but steady growth of the post-1983 U.S. economy will continue for the next decade and a half; the second, called the Cycle forecast, assumes that the U.S. economy will experience periodic but relatively mild recessions in 1992 and 1997. While the two forecasts are not dramatically different in the long run, the Cycle forecast shows higher rates of inflation, higher interest rates, and slower real GNP growth than does the Trend forecast. As a result, the Cycle forecast represents a more pessimistic, less stable future for American families.[3]

As table 7.1 shows, the growth in average real hourly earnings, which we use to proxy overall earnings growth, is only about 40 to 50 percent of what it was in the 1950s and 1960s.[4] Furthermore, even under the Trend forecast, the more optimistic scenario, real growth in the Gross National Product (GNP) is only about half of what it was during the 1960s and prices grow at a rate that is 50 percent more than in the 1960s and almost five times more than in the 1950s. Finally, the unemployment rates in the Trend forecast are higher at all stages of the business cycle than in either of those prior decades.

The DRI forecasts show potential economies in the 1990s that are significantly stronger and more stable than the 1973–1983 U.S. economy, but significantly weaker in most aspects than the economies of the 1950s and 1960s. In general, these forecasts lead to economies that are more similar to that of the 1983–1988 period than to those of any other post-World War II period.

The DRI forecasts do not address the issue of wealth or debt growth among households and families. But given the similarity in these

Table 7.1 COMPARISONS OF KEY ECONOMIC VARIABLES, 1953–2000
           (percent)

Economic variable	1953–63	1963–73	1973–83	DRI forecasts 1990–2000	
				Trend	Cycle
Total change in Consumer Price Index	+ 14.5	+ 45.1	+ 109.3	+ 66.8	+ 74.6
Average annual growth rate in real GNP	+ 3.1	+ 4.6	+ 1.9	2.3	1.9
Total change in real average hourly earnings	+ 19.4	+ 19.8	− 3.0	+ 11.6	+ 10.1
Range of the rate of unemployment	2.9–6.8	3.5–5.9	4.5–9.7	5.2–5.8	4.9–8.0

Source: 1953–1983 data from the Economic Report of the President (January 1989) except for the 1973–83 Consumer Price Index change, which is the CPI-x1 change from the U.S. Congressional Budget Office (1988). Forecast data from Data Resources, Inc. (1989).

Table 7.2 AVERAGE ANNUAL REAL RATES OF RETURN ON SELECTED
           INVESTMENTS, 1953–1988
           (percent)

Period	New home[a]	Stocks[b]	3-year Treasury notes
1953–62	3.3	8.5	1.4
1962–73	4.2	− 1.0	1.9
1973–83	1.0	− 2.2	1.8
1983–88	5.0	7.9	5.5

Note: All figures deflated by the PCE deflator.
a. As measured by the increase in the median sales price of a new home.
b. As measured by the growth in the total Dow Jones Index.

forecasts to the U.S. economy between 1983 and 1988, it is instructive to look at how key elements in net wealth growth have fared over this period.

To do this, we return to the three proxy measures for growth in family net wealth originally shown in table 5.8. In table 7.2, the growth in real median home values is used to approximate the growth in the value of all homes. The real growth in the Dow Jones total index is used to approximate the growth in the value of equities. And the interest rate on three-year Treasury notes is used to approximate the return on interest-bearing investments such as bonds, savings accounts, certificates of deposits, and money market accounts.

As the figures in table 7.2 show, the period from 1983 through 1988 was an extraordinary one for these three indicators. The real value of homes rose at an average annual rate that is nearly a percentage point higher than the 1960s, the best previous period in our study. Equity growth far outstripped the stagnant annual averages of the 20-year period from 1962 to 1983 and approached the halcyon years of the 1950s. This occurred in spite of the major stock market collapse in October 1987. Finally, real interest rates as represented in the three-year treasury bond rate reached a sustained annual average that appears to be a post-World War II high.

The implications for family net wealth growth are clear from our previous discussion in chapter 5. Families who own their own homes, who have invested in equities markets, or who have cash to deposit in interest-bearing accounts will fare quite well in this kind of environment. Families who are non-home owners, who have significant amounts of interest-sensitive debt or who have only small amounts of liquid assets will fare poorly. This generally means that in an economic environment similar to the current one or those represented by the DRI forecasts, younger families will not do as well as older families with respect to net wealth.

In table 7.3 we look at selected ownership rates by age group from the 1986 Survey of Consumer Expenditures, taken roughly at the midpoint year of the 1983–1988 economic recovery. As the table

Table 7.3 RATES OF HOME AND ASSET OWNERSHIP AND INDEBTEDNESS BY AGE GROUP IN 1986

	Percent owning or holding				
Age group	Homes	Liquid assets >$5000	Mortgage debt[a]	Other debt[b]	Other debt >$5000
25–34	42	42	95	69	24
35–44	64	63	86	78	32
45–54	78	61	68	70	28
55–64	75	64	43	58	17
65 +	73	59	19	27	4

Source: Urban Institute tabulations from the 1986 Survey of Consumer Finances.
a. This column represents the percentage of homeowners who have mortgages.
b. Other debt includes all non-real-estate debt such as credit card balances.

shows, families with heads between 25 and 34 (roughly born in the 1950s) were less likely to own their own homes, more likely to have mortgage debt if they did own their own homes, and less likely to have significant financial assets than families with older heads. As a result, these families were on average not in a position to take advantage of historically high real interest rates or the rapid appreciation in housing values and equities. In fact, high interest rates coupled with rising home prices probably acted as a barrier to their entrance into the housing market. We return to this subject later.

On the other hand, families with heads who were 55 or older, that is, those born before 1931, were well-positioned to increase their net wealth holdings. More than three-quarters of them owned their own homes, and among these homeowners, less than 35 percent still had mortgages to pay off. Almost two-thirds owned liquid assets in excess of $5,000 and, although it is not shown in the table, more than 40 percent had liquid assets in excess of $20,000. Significantly fewer of them had any form of debt (other than mortgages) and of those that did, more than 80 percent had total other debt under $5,000.

As of 1986, therefore, it appears that as a group, older families continued to lend money to younger families, and because rates of return to loans were so high in real terms, they could substantially increase their net wealth in the prospect.[5] If either of the two DRI economic scenarios for the 1990s proves true, this relationship is likely to continue in the foreseeable future, which contrasts dramatically with the 1950s and 1960s, the period when the parents and older siblings of baby boomers were just starting out, when real interest rates were low, and housing appreciation strong. So although the economy in the post-1983 period and the economic forecast for the 1990s represent significant improvements over the economy of the 1970s, these improvements are most likely to benefit those who are already financially secure.

Thus, in the next decade younger families are not going to be as fortunate as the two generations that immediately preceded them. High equity prices mean they are unlikely to find ways to increase their net wealth holdings in the stock market unless they already have substantial holdings. And because, as a group, they tend to be borrowers rather than lenders, the high real interest rates will work to their disadvantage in financial markets.

As we pointed out earlier, the cornerstone of net wealth for the average family in the past 40 years has been the family home. Given this gloomy picture, should and can families continue to make sacrifices to buy their own home in the decade to come? We examine the prospects for the housing market in the next section.

THE PROSPECTS FOR HOUSING AFFORDABILITY AND APPRECIATION

As we discussed in chapter 5, home equity is the single most important component of net wealth for the more than two-thirds of all families who live in a home they own. For many families, home equity accounts for well more than half of their net wealth (see table 5.12). For these families, the ability to enter the housing market and experience appreciation in home values during their period of ownership has been critical to the growth in their financial security.

We have already shown that in the years since 1983, the appreciation in home values has been at historically high levels nationally.[6] At the same time, real interest rates have also been very high, much higher than in any of the three previous decades. Finally, the bulk of the baby boom generation has already matured into its home buying years, and thus in the 1990s the number of new units required to house future populations is expected to drop dramatically from the levels of the 1970s and 1980s.

These factors create a very different housing market from the one that existed prior to 1983. The current market is one in which there is greater uncertainty about housing affordability and housing appreciation. Two questions are central to the future importance of home equity in the net wealth of today's baby boomers. Will young families be able to afford to buy their first home at prevailing prices and interest rates? Will homes appreciate in value if the demand for new housing declines substantially?

The housing affordability issue has been the subject of several recent papers.[7] As noted earlier, the cost of paying the principal and interest on a median-priced house for a lone young male wage earner rose from 15–16 percent of income in the 1950s and 1960s to 40 percent or more in the 1980s. Even if we account for the fact that many young families have two wage earners, the increase in housing costs for families is dramatic. The percentage of a young family's income necessary to pay the principal and interest on a new home rose from 15–16 percent in the 1950s and 1960s to 28 percent in the 1980s. Anthony Downs reports that property taxes would add another 4 percentage points to that latter figure in 1988.[8]

Leonard et al. have shown that the affordability problem is even more severe among lower income families. The authors report that in 1985 almost 40 percent of homeowners who were poor spent 60 percent or more of their income on housing, and another 25 percent spent between 35 and 65 percent of their income on housing.[9] Both of these percentages were substantially higher than in the late 1970s.

In spite of these dismal statistics, young families in the early 1980s managed roughly to maintain ownership rates. In 1985 the Harvard-MIT Joint Center for Housing Studies reported that between 1979 and 1983, the percentage of young households (heads less than age 35) owning their own homes only declined from 43 to 42 percent.[10] A more recent Joint Center study reports that the declines have continued but at a rate that seems slow relative to the dramatic changes in affordability. Among families with heads less than 25, home ownership rates declined from 19 percent in 1983 to 16 percent in 1988. But among families with heads ages 25–34, home ownership rates only declined from 47 percent in 1983 to 45 percent in 1988.[11] This slight rate of decline was evident across households of all types: married with children, married without children, single parent, single person. Thus, while home ownership rates among persons under age 35 are significantly lower than the rates in the early to mid-1970s, they seem to have stabilized in the mid-1980s. It is even more remarkable that these recent changes have been so modest, because they occurred during a period when the costs of ownership were rising substantially and the tax incentives for home ownership were reduced significantly by the federal income tax rate reductions contained in the Tax Reform Act of 1986.

This reinforces our argument that individuals continue to believe that home ownership is worth significant sacrifices. But can young families continue to make financial sacrifices and increase their incomes enough to enter the housing market? If they can, will housing prices continue to rise, thus making such sacrifices worthwhile? Responses to these questions are complex and not all observers agree on potential future impacts of economics and demographics. We try to make sense of the various arguments in the following discussion.

N. Gregory Mankiw and David N. Weil of the National Bureau of Economic Research, using a relatively simple model that does not account for local market variations, argue:

> The entry of the Baby Boom generation into its house-buying years is ... the major cause of the increase in real housing prices in the 1970s. Since the Baby Bust generation is now entering its house-buying years, housing demand will grow more slowly in the 1990s than

in any time in the past forty years. If the historical relation between housing demand and housing prices continues into the future, real housing prices will fall substantially over the next two decades.[12]

Mankiw and Weil estimate that in the next 20 years the real value of housing nationally will decline by 3 percent per year. Even the most optimistic (and admittedly least realistic) version of their model estimates that housing values will rise at rates that are less than a third of the increases experienced in the 1970s.

Mankiw and Weil temper their results with several caveats, and certainly foresee no collapse in the housing market. First, there is much uncertainty about future housing prices because of macro-economic conditions and local housing variations. Second, in spite of lower tax rates there remain tax and psychological advantages to home ownership that will probably not change dramatically in the next decade. Finally, there is unlikely to be a large sell-off of homes because a large majority of families currently own their own homes and have substantial equity in them. The need to pay considerable capital gains taxes on that equity is an important deterrent to the wholesale dumping of residential housing units on the market.

Downs also argues that a collapse in the housing market in the next 20 years is unlikely:

> [U.S.] . . . median home prices rarely have declined in any region since 1966, despite the three recessions that have occurred since that time . . . In real estate markets in general and housing markets in par-ticular, sales prices tend to fall precipitously only when there is a **sudden and massive withdrawal of demand for space** . . . Such an immense oversupply rarely occurs . . . because annual additions to the housing inventory are small compared with its total size . . . Hence, fears of catastrophic general economic consequences caused by sharply falling home prices are grossly exaggerated, to say the least.[13]

Downs points out, however, that prosperity in local economies can lead to perverse housing market effects. When a specific area ex-periences rising employment, population, and income, both housing demand and housing prices increase. The dilemma is that such areas also need to attract workers at all wage levels to fill the new jobs being created. But historically, such areas tend to adopt tighter re-strictions against both commercial and residential building in an effort to alleviate such pains of growth as traffic congestion. These restrictions push housing prices even higher because they restrict supply in the face of rising demand.[14]

The result can be that the areas of a nation where jobs are most plentiful will not have an adequate supply of housing that is affordable to the workers who potentially might fill those jobs. Downs notes that such situations in England, Japan, and West Germany have resulted in workers in depressed areas where there are higher unemployment rates being unable to afford to move to booming areas where there are acute labor shortages and resulting high home prices. While the United States has not seen labor demand and supply mismatches of the magnitude of Europe and Japan, anecdotal evidence is beginning to emerge that corporate workers now consider housing costs to be a major factor in deciding whether to accept a transfer from one area to another.

As Downs also notes, in areas that have weak employment growth, the reverse often occurs. Local jurisdictions loosen real estate development restrictions, essentially depressing the growth in housing prices and making it more difficult for current home owners to sell and realize significant financial gains.

The fastest solution to housing price acceleration for high growth areas would be a "severe economic recession."[15] But, as Downs observes, "favoring a recession to ease [these] problems . . . would be foolish given the immense social costs . . ."[16] Furthermore, our own affordability calculations imply that immediately following the 1982–1983 recession, rapidly declining real interest rates were accompanied by rapidly accelerating real housing prices, resulting in very little improvement in housing affordability.

What do these varying judgments imply for the future of American families with respect to reliance on home ownership to build their own net wealth? While the complexities of housing markets and their interactions with economic and social trends make precise forecasting impossible, several general points seem clear:

☐ In the 1990s, because of the demographics of the baby bust, national housing prices and consequently home equity in the U.S. are unlikely to continue their rapid growth rate of the past decade and a half. Thus, although we are unlikely to experience a wholesale collapse in prices, appreciation rates will slow considerably.

☐ Some high economic growth areas will experience housing price increases that not only exceed the national averages but exceed the rate of family income growth. Furthermore, in such areas, the perverse effects mentioned by Downs may lead to a housing market that effectively excludes lower income families from home ownership and creates serious local labor supply shortages in industries dependent on middle and lower income workers.

□ Given these perverse effects in high growth areas, current home owners will continue to accrue home equity driven by rising home prices. Those families who have not been able to enter the housing market before rapid price acceleration began, however, may be excluded for the foreseeable future. This will create widening gaps in net wealth between home owners and renters.

□ In a corollary fashion, low growth areas will experience very little housing price growth and may experience some declines. Home equity in such areas will increase much more slowly than the national average and may increase only by the amount of principal being repaid. In these areas, the slow growth of home equity will minimize net wealth gaps between home owners and renters.

□ A national or local recession of considerable magnitude could act to alleviate housing price growth as well as bring down interest rates. But the resulting income losses could be of such magnitude that we would not see any improvement in housing affordability. Interest rate declines spurred by changes in federal monetary or fiscal policy that do not cause an economic downturn would help housing affordability in the short run, but could also lead to an acceleration in home prices in high growth areas.

Except for those families in consistently high growth areas of the country, therefore, home ownership cannot be relied upon to drive a family's net wealth growth in the next decade. Coupled with our previous conclusion that general economic growth is not likely to lead to income gains on a par with the 1950s and 1960s, this leaves only two potential sources of net wealth growth: changes in savings, debt, and consumption behavior; and inheritances. We discuss each of these in turn.

TRENDS IN PERSONAL SAVINGS AND DEBT: AMERICAN BEHAVIORAL CHANGES

Many factors can affect the accumulation of net wealth over individual lifetimes. In recent years, two of these factors, savings and debt, have received some attention because it has been argued that major shifts in behavior related to them have taken place.

Savings

In the case of savings it is widely believed that the national savings rate has declined significantly beginning in the 1970s but accelerating in the 1980s.[17] The total U.S. savings rate has fallen from an average of 8 percent of net national product between 1950 and 1979 to an average of 2 percent in the 1980s.[18] As with many economic variables, the savings rate can be measured in a variety of ways, but all measures lead to the same conclusion. Real savings per worker, for example, declined by 12 percent between 1973 (its peak) and 1983.

In 1988 Michael Boskin, currently chairman of President Bush's Council of Economic Advisers, and Lawrence Lau reported that there may be a generational effect in savings behavior. They note:

> . . . [an] apparent tremendous difference in the propensity to save by
> households headed by persons born pre and post 1939, *at the same
> age.* It appears that as the share of total national resources held by
> persons born post 1939 rises, the national savings rate will decrease
> unless some major modifications occur in the consumption/wealth
> patterns at later ages for persons born post 1939. . .[19]

If sustained over a long period of time, these reported declines in the savings rate can depress investment and growth in the national economy. They can also slow the accumulation of net wealth among families.

The Boskin and Lau analyses used data only through 1980. Has there been any shift in savings behavior among young families since that time?

Generally, individuals and families define savings in a more limited way than do the studies cited here. Most analyses of savings behavior by economists include private pension contributions made by employers that are not available to the employee until retirement. Some include unrealized capital gains in corporate equities. And national savings includes both business savings and government surpluses or deficits. Individuals and families are more likely to think of savings as the amount of disposable (after-tax) income they do not spend.

If we use the more limited definition of savings, that is, the percentage of disposable income not spent, there is some evidence that there has been a shift since the early 1980s. Table 7.4 shows tabulations for various years from the Bureau of Labor Statistics' Consumer Expenditure Surveys. Aggregate figures also show an

Table 7.4 SAVINGS BEHAVIOR IN THE 1980s

Families headed by	Percent of disposable income saved		
a person age	1973	1981	1986
25–34	4	1	4
35–44	4	1	5
45–54	10	6	−2
55–64	12	9	7
65+	6	−6	0

Source: *U.S. Department of Labor, Bureau of Labor Statistics News: Consumer Expenditure Surveys*, results from years indicated. Tables are from the annual interview surveys.

improvement in personal savings after 1985. But the government deficit is still depressing total national savings.

These data show that the percentage of disposable income saved declined significantly among families, irrespective of age, between 1973 and 1981; this is consistent with the findings of the other authors just discussed. In fact, among elderly families there appeared to be some significant dissavings in 1981. By 1986, however, savings ratios among younger families matched or exceeded (in the case of the 35- to 44-year-old group) those of 1973. The ratio also improved for elderly families, although the ratios for families headed by persons between 45 and 64 appeared to deteriorate further.

These more recent trends tend to contradict the Boskin and Lau conclusions about the post-1939 cohorts. At least in 1986, lower savings ratios and dissavings appeared to be confined to those generations born *prior to 1941*. Indeed, aggregate data for 1988 and 1989 show a small increase in personal savings, perhaps presaging a more sustained long-run rebound in savings behavior.[20]

Debt

Turning now to the issue of debt growth, we find some positive developments among today's younger families. There have been many media articles about the rise in household debt or personal liabilities as measured by data from the Federal Reserve's Flow of Funds accounts. As reported earlier in table 5.2, for example, real personal liabilities per household grew dramatically during the 1960s, though that growth tapered off somewhat during the 1970s. The net result of this growth, however, has been that both cumulative liabilities per household and the ratio of personal liabilities to personal income have reached historical highs in the 1980s (table 7.5). In 1983, aggregate personal liabilities totaled 93 percent of aggregate personal income, more than twice as high as at the start of the 1950s.

A popular misconception, previously held by us and others, is that this debt growth has occurred largely among younger members of society who are spending beyond their means. Our current findings indicate that this may not be the case.

The analysis of the growth of personal debt is often based on various relationships between debt and income. This makes intuitive sense because debt is normally paid off from income flows. If the ratio of debt to income is abnormally high, the ability to repay debt quickly is questionable. This applies to households and families as well as to nations, and may be particularly true in recent periods when real interest rates on debt have been high. But an alternative way to look at debt is in relation to net wealth. This is often how experts evaluate the financial health of business organizations. The guiding principal is to ensure that in the event liquidation is necessary, the value of assets is sufficient to pay off outstanding debt.

The data we have developed from the various studies and surveys cited earlier allow us to calculate the ratio between debt and net wealth by age group over the last three decades. These calculations, shown in table 7.6, indicate a more positive picture than is shown in the aggregate debt/income ratios in table 7.5.

The ratio of debt to net wealth appears to have peaked sometime in the 1960s for families of all ages. As we would expect, younger families have the highest ratios, but the young families of the 1980s actually have lower ratios than those of the 1960s and 1970s. In 1986, for example, families with heads ages 25–34 had debt that totaled

Table 7.5 GROWTH IN PERSONAL LIABILITIES

Year	Real per household liabilities (1987 dollars)	Ratio of personal liabilities to personal income
1949	9,268	.41
1959	18,560	.66
1969	28,753	.79
1972	31,519	.84
1983	36,071	.93

Source: Authors' calculations from the Federal Reserve Board's Flow of Funds data (for personal liabilities); the Commerce Department Bureau of Economic Analysis National Income Account data (for personal income); and various Census P-60 reports for household data.

Table 7.6 RATIO OF FAMILY DEBT TO FAMILY NET WEALTH

Families headed by a person age	Ratio of family debt to family net wealth				
	1953	1962	1979	1983	1986
25–34	.34	.66	.58	.50	.53
35–44	.22	.46	.29	.29	.36
45–54	.09	.23	.11	.15	.15
55–64	.06	.15	.04	.02	.03
65 +	.04	.05	.04	.02	.03
All families	.13	.27	.17	.14	.16

Source: 1953 and 1962: 1953 Survey of Consumer Finances and 1962 Survey of the Financial Characteristics of Consumers, in Katona et al. (1963); 1979: 1979 Income Survey Development Program file, in Radner and Vaughn (1984); 1983 and 1986: tabulations by the authors from the 1983 and 1986 Surveys of Consumer Finances.

53 percent of their net wealth. Family heads of similar age in 1962 and 1979 had ratios of 66 and 58 percent, respectively. The decline in these ratios since the 1960s has been universal across all age groups, although the three age groups between 35 and 64 appear to have experienced a modest increase or only a small decline in their ratios since the late 1970s.[21]

The figures in table 7.6 suggest that families may be conscious about growing debt and may not have allowed their own debt to grow as quickly as their net wealth. Although a national economic catastrophe would limit the ability of all families to cash in their assets to pay off their debt simultaneously, it does appear that most families would be able to remain solvent even if forced to reduce their personal debt. Like our savings examples, this micro-level view gives us a more positive picture of the economic viability of American families than do the aggregate data.

The Implications

Even if families are conscious of their growing debt and taking steps accordingly, most economists agree that recent low savings rates in the United States create some serious long-term financial and economic problems for the economy as a whole:

> In the short run this splurge of consumption spending (both public and private) has had some beneficial effects of stimulating a sustained strong recovery from the 1982 recession; but, increasingly, the pleasures of the spending binge are being tempered by a recognition of its costs: a loss of world markets, reduced future growth prospects, and increased debt burdens on future generations.[22]

We earlier quoted the Boskin and Lau (1988) findings of a strong generational effect in savings and consumption behavior—with persons born after 1939 showing a lower tendency to save and a higher tendency to consume than persons born before 1939. These authors argue that the currently low savings rates may move even lower if the cohort behavioral phenomenon continues.[23] We have shown that more recent figures suggest a reversal of this pattern since 1980, the most recent data available to Boskin and Lau. The question becomes, has the reversal of the previous pattern been enough to compensate for the aggregate effects of the savings and consumption behavior in the 1970s?

Table 7.7 shows annual average changes in per worker and per capita savings and consumption over the decades since World War II. As we noted earlier, both consumption and savings were rising rapidly during the 1950s and 1960s.[24] In the 1970s, consumption growth did not stop but slowed considerably; savings actually declined under both measures. Since 1983, per *worker* savings has continued to decline and per worker consumption has accelerated only modestly. Per *capita* savings and consumption have both experienced more substantial turnarounds, but the differences appear to have been caused by a proportionally larger increase in employment among single workers.[25] Thus, the per capita figures show the effects of demographic distortions, because fixed consumption items such as rent tend to make the per capita consumption of a single individual higher than that of a couple or family.

These figures imply that the improvement in savings behavior since 1983 has not been sufficient to correct for the dramatic declines experienced during the 1970s. Furthermore, consumption seems to be increasing at significantly higher rates than in the 1970s, implying

Table 7.7 CHANGES IN REAL SAVINGS AND CONSUMPTION, 1953–1988
(Average annual compounded rates of change)
(percent)

Period	Savings		Consumption	
	Per worker	Per capita	Per worker	Per capita
1953–63	+ 1.1	+ .4	+ 2.0	+ 1.6
1963–73	+ 6.5	+ 8.3	+ 2.3	+ 3.6
1973–83	− 1.2	− .6	+ .8	+ 1.5
1983–88	− .9	+ .9	+ 1.2	+ 3.0

Source: Calculated by the authors from savings, consumption, labor force, and population data from U.S. Council of Economic Advisers (1989).

that the imbalance between spending and saving has worsened since economic recovery began in 1983. On the basis of this, and given that economic growth in the 1990s will look very much like that of the 1983–1988 period, are we to conclude that savings and consumption behavior will not change for the better in the near future? Are Boskin and Lau correct about the possibility that the cohort effect will increase the misalignment in savings and consumption patterns in the longer run?

The answers to these questions are uncertain, but here are our speculations. First, the national per worker savings and consumption data through 1988 indicate that there will be no spontaneous turnabout in individual behavior. Policy changes during the 1983–1988 period did not seem to help, even when accompanied by sustained growth in incomes and historically high real interest rates. By 1988, for example, reduced income tax rates and the loss of non-mortgage interest deductibility implemented as part of the Tax Reform Act of 1986 might have been expected to increase savings. All other things being equal, this legislation increased disposable income and substantially reduced the tax advantages associated with credit buying. Yet per worker savings continued to fall, and per worker consumption increased at an average rate 50 percent higher than in the 1970s. There seem to be no policy changes or economic events on the horizon that would be dramatic enough to induce changes in this behavior.

Second, this problem may not, in fact, get worse in the future as the post-1939 cohort that Boskin and Lau identify comes to dominate the population of workers and consumers. In table 7.4, data from the Bureau of Labor Statistics' Consumer Expenditure Survey indicates that young families in 1986 had increased their savings rates (and correspondingly decreased their consumption rates) relative to the early 1980s. By this measure, the 1986 savings rates of families with heads under age 45 equaled or exceeded the rates for similar young families in the early 1970s, the period just before the economic slowdown of the 1970s and 1980s. In fact, the figures from table 7.4 show that it is the older families who seem to have decreased their savings relative to the 1970s. This contradicts traditional views of lifetime consumption and savings patterns, but it may be a byproduct of the fact that most older families own their own homes and have considerable equity in them. This could give them a net wealth cushion large enough to make them feel comfortable increasing their consumption in their pre-retirement years.

What does this imply for the growth in family net wealth? In general, an increase in savings of younger families will add substantially to the net wealth of a family over time. Even a simple calculation with an assumption of no increase in real income shows how dramatic this difference can be by the time a young person today reaches retirement. For example, if a family with a head age 30 who earns the mean income in 1987 (about $31,000) saved 1 percent of its income every year (the savings rate for such families in 1981), they would have accumulated only about $19,000 in 1987 dollars by the time the head reached age 65.[26] If the same family saved 4 percent of its income (the savings rate for such families in 1986 in table 7.4), the accumulation would be about $75,000. Thus, a sustained and significant increase in the savings rates of families would not only improve the national savings and investment rates, but would considerably enhance the net wealth of individual families.

Thus, if younger families continue to save at higher rates than older families (table 7.4), we may in fact see the exact inverse of what Boskin and Lau have suggested: as the post-1939 generation becomes a larger proportion of the U.S. working population, savings rates may actually increase. We must, however, treat these figures with some caution because they need to be confirmed by more recent consumer expenditure and personal savings data that are not yet available. Furthermore, the general trends in savings and consumption shown in table 7.7 for the period 1983–1988 imply that families have recently increased consumption faster than savings. If this behavior crosses generations, the positive developments in savings among young families indicated in table 7.4 may reverse themselves.

BABY BOOMERS AND INHERITANCES

There is a popular misconception that many working persons today, especially baby boomers from middle-class families, will inherit significant sums of money, thus do not need to save or invest because their parents have already done that for them.[27] But the evidence to support this belief is thin. It is true, as we have argued in chapter 5, that the generation of baby boomers' parents seem to be quite fortunate with respect to their net wealth growth. They will probably reach retirement in the late 1990s with an average net wealth that exceeds any prior or succeeding generation now alive. But will they leave any or all of these funds to their children?

There is a lively debate among economists about the presence of a bequest motive among older persons.[28] Kotlikoff and Summers (1981) have argued that intergenerational transfers account for approximately four-fifths of the nation's wealth. Other analysts have used household-level data to show that elderly persons actually save rather than dissave, and that this tendency increases at older ages.[29] After eliminating alternative rational explanations, analysts use the motive to bequeath some sum of money to heirs to explain this savings increase as individuals approach their deaths.

But efforts to prove empirically the existence of a bequest motive using data that follow individual families and persons over time have not been successful. Michael Hurd, using one of the household-level surveys most appropriate for this kind of analysis, reports:

> There is no evidence for a bequest motive, at least insofar as it depends on whether the household has living children. This does not necessarily mean that parents do not care about the welfare of their children. In fact, the wealth data suggest that parents transfer substantial wealth to their children, but, as would be suggested by a standard human capital model, it is transferred earlier in life to support the children's consumption and education.[30]

In other words, it is likely that most intergenerational transfers of wealth are made well before the death of both parents and should be reflected in the net wealth or, in the case of transfers for higher education, in the income of the children. Under this hypothesis, by 1983 and 1986 most baby boomers may have already been the recipients of the bulk of the parental transfers they will receive in their lifetime.

One argument that can be made to counter this is that parents may overestimate the amount of net wealth they need to support themselves from retirement to death, thus leaving wealth to their children inadvertently. But, as Hurd points out, the existence of significant sums of net wealth among the retired today does not guarantee that an estate will be left tomorrow even if mortality rates are considerably lower than expected. The maintenance and growth of net wealth values are dependent on random events such as the health status of the parents and the returns on various assets. A parent who heavily invested in the stock market in October 1987, for example, might have lost considerable portions of the net wealth reported on the 1986 Survey of Consumer Finances (SCF). A parent who develops a debilitating illness such as Alzheimer's disease could deplete large sums of net wealth long before death. And even the data we show from the 1986 Consumer Expenditure Survey (table 7.4) indicate that families with heads over 45 are on average dissaving rather than saving.

Data from the 1986 SCF confirm that inheritances have not been an important element in the net wealth portfolio of families in the past, nor are they expected to be in the future. Only 7 percent of families reported that most of their net wealth at that time came from inheritances or gifts, and only 14 percent said they ever expected to receive large inheritances. More than 80 percent said they definitely did not expect to receive large inheritances in the future.

The conclusion we reach is that dependence upon significant inheritances by a large number of today's young families is probably not prudent. Some young families will undoubtedly benefit from the good will and good luck of their older relatives. But they will not be numerous enough to alter the net wealth status of their cohort relative to other cohorts.

THE OUTLOOK FOR BABY BOOMERS

In practice, we know that many factors can dramatically affect the wealth holdings and future prospects of any generation. Not all of these can be measured using surveys and forecasts such as the ones in this book. Poor investment choices, illness, even the structure of local housing markets can help or hinder the net wealth growth of individuals and families. In the sections above we have shown how general economic and housing trends projected for the future will act to depress the growth in the net wealth of today's young families relative to previous generations. We have also argued that while inherited money may help some of these young families, inheritances will not be numerous or substantial enough to make a significant difference for the whole generation. On the more positive side, we have shown that young families near the middle of the income distribution could substantially improve their net wealth at retirement by increasing their savings rates.

It is beyond the scope of the current effort to control for all the factors that are important in projecting what might happen in the future. But we can get a notion of a worst case scenario by using a method roughly comparable to the wage projections presented in chapter 6. We know that the future is not likely to be as bad as this scenario envisions, because the U.S. economic experience since 1983 and the one expected in the 1990s are much more positive than that of the 1973–1983 period. But the results will tell us about the lower bound expectations on net wealth that young families may experience.

We begin by assuming that baby boomers continue to experience a proportionally lower growth *rate* in their net wealth relative to the growth experienced by their parents' generation. What level of net wealth will they have when they reach retirement? Will it be significantly lower than that of their parents' generation? How will it compare to the net wealth of their grandparents' generation, a group now well into its retirement years and seemingly doing well?

Table 7.8 contains the results of these lower bound net wealth calculations for baby boomers and the actual net wealth of two previous generations at similar ages.[31] Under these projections, the entire cohort of baby boomers will reach retirement (ages 55–64) with less than 50 percent of the net wealth of their parents' cohort at a similar age: $143,000 versus $293,000.

Is the baby boom generation as a group doomed to an impoverished retirement as a result of this? Not if you look at the data more closely. First, we must remember that the cohort we use to represent the parents of baby boomers has had extraordinarily good financial fortune throughout its working life. This group's progress may have erroneously become the standard measure of financial success for its children and subsequent generations. More realistically, this group's success is the very lucky exception to the history of family net wealth growth and may not be the most appropriate standard by which baby boomers should measure their progress. The same is true of the intervening cohort (1939–1948): they had the good fortune to mature when U.S. economic growth was quite robust.

Second, any generation that was financially mature in the boom periods of the 1950s or 1960s appears to have fared reasonably well (the cohort of 1929–1938 was financially mature in *both* decades). The members of the baby boom generation have at least two more decades in their financial life cycle, and circumstances may turn sufficiently in their favor to restore growth rates in their net wealth. If either of those decades is one of strong economic growth, they might expect the growth of their net wealth to match those of previous generations. Although it does not currently appear that such a boom will occur in the 1990s, it is conceivable that the early part of the 21st century could be a period of strong economic growth in the United States, particularly if federal deficit and international trade problems are resolved by that time. And, as discussed in the

Table 7.8 ACTUAL AND PROJECTED NET WEALTH OF THREE GENERATIONS, 1962–2013

	1962	1973	1983	1993	2003	2013
Grandparents (born 1909–1918)						
Net wealth (000s of dollars)	114	157	205	n/a	n/a	n/a
Approximate age (years)	45–54	55–64	65+			
Parents (born 1929–1938)						
Net wealth (000s of dollars)	38	118	212	293	384	n/a
Approximate age (years)	25–34	35–44	45–54	55–64	65+	
Baby boomers (born 1949–58)						
Net wealth (000s of dollars)	n/a	n/a	44	64	105	143
Approximate age (years)	5–14	15–24	25–34	35–44	45–54	55–64
Education group						
Net wealth (000s of dollars)						
≤ High school	n/a	n/a	30	44	71	97
≥ Some college	n/a	n/a	49	72	128	176

Source: Values for 1962–1983 are drawn from Greenwood and Wolff (1988); values for 1993–2013 are projected by the authors.
n/a = not available or not calculated by the authors.

savings section above, a change in savings and consumption behavior by baby boomers will most certainly increase the growth rates in their net wealth beyond those assumed in table 7.8.

Finally, even if real net wealth growth during their working lives remains at proportionally the same low level, baby boomers will still reach retirement age with only about 9 percent less net wealth than persons on the verge of retirement in 1973 ($143,000 versus $157,000). In more general terms, average baby boomers will be in only a slightly worse financial position than their grandparents' cohort (1909–1918). And, from all that we have observed, members of the cohort of 1909–1918 have fared reasonably well during their retirement years, albeit at a somewhat more modest level of existence than their children (born 1929–1938) will experience during retirement.

But these positive notes will not apply equally to all members of the young middle class today. The future prospects for both wage growth and home ownership among the lesser educated young do not seem as good at this time. Lack of wage growth will severely limit the ability of young families to increase their savings and enter the housing market. And while home ownership in the 1990s is unlikely to guarantee strong net wealth growth, it almost certainly is necessary to insulate families from rapid escalations in housing costs, especially in high growth areas. As the projections in table 7.8 indicate, even assuming (optimistically) that the less educated have proportionally the same net wealth growth rate as the more educated, they would reach retirement with net wealth that was 40 percent lower than the more educated.

The bottom line is that today's young will probably not experience a growth or level of net wealth comparable to those of their parents. This will be particularly true of those young persons with a high school education or less. But even under the most pessimistic scenario, the better educated among them are likely to live as well in retirement as the elderly of today.

Notes

1. It is possible that ongoing Surveys of Consumer Finances and the future availability of longitudinal wealth data from surveys such as the Census Bureau's Survey of Income and Program Participation (SIPP) and the University of Michigan's Panel Study on Income Dynamics (PSID) will improve our ability to develop such models within the next few years.

2. See Data Resources, Inc. (1989).

3. It should be noted that each of these forecasts is roughly comparable to the high and low labor productivity assumptions used in the previous chapter. The 1.9 percent productivity path used in the father-son income projections, however, is somewhat more optimistic than the Trend forecast here. We could not use the Trend forecast in chapter 6, because DRI does not project labor productivity increases in sufficient historical detail.

4. In general, income growth exceeds the growth rate in average hourly earnings because earnings constitute only one portion, albeit an important one, of total family income.

5. Of course, the borrowing-lending market is not limited to intra-U.S. exchanges. A significant amount of the money that Americans borrow now comes from foreign owners of capital.

6. Clearly, there is substantial variation among local housing markets. Housing prices in oil-producing states such as Texas and Louisiana have suffered since the decline in oil prices began in the early 1980s, while housing prices in the Northeast and California have risen at sometimes astounding rates. But this is almost always related to general economic prosperity in a specific area, so growing or shrinking housing prices are often associated with rising or falling incomes. In general, the relationship between average housing prices and average incomes in specific local markets moves in similar, though perhaps not proportional, directions to the national measures of affordability used here and by other authors. The slowing of general U.S. economic growth in late 1990, for example, led to an almost universal decline in the growth of house values across the nation.

7. See Levy and Michel (1986), Downs (1989), Leonard, Dolbeare and Lazere (1989), and Joint Center for Housing Studies (1985 and 1989).

8. See Downs (1989), p. 7.

9. Leonard, Dolbeare and Lazere (1989), p. 5.

10. Joint Center for Housing Studies (1985), p. 11.

11. Joint Center for Housing Studies (1989), p. 32.

12. Mankiw and Weil (1988), p. ii.

13. Downs (1989), pp. 14–15.

14. Downs, p. 12.

15. Ibid., p. 12.

16. Ibid., p. 12.

17. For good overviews of this phenomenon, see U.S. Council of Economic Advisers (1990), chapter 4, and Hendershott (1985).

18. See Bosworth (1988) for a lucid discussion of this particular measure and its consequences.

19. Boskin and Lau (1988), p. 63.

20. We should note that analysis of savings behavior is complex, and it is beyond the scope of this book to undertake a systematic treatment.

21. For example, Edward Wolff has noted in a private communication to The Urban Institute that debt to net wealth ratios generated from the national balance sheets do not confirm a rise in the ratios from 1953 to 1962. Like analysis of savings, analysis of debt is complicated and it is beyond the scope of this book to discuss the implications of these findings in detail.

22. Bosworth, p. 1.

23. Boskin and Lau, pp. 76–77.

24. The differences in these two decades reflect the demographic effects of family size changes occurring during these periods. In the 1950s, with birth rates high and rising because of the baby boom, per capita figures were rising more slowly than per worker figures. In the 1960s, with the baby boom ending, the reverse is true. Once again, this points to the importance of accounting for individual demographic adjustments in interpreting the direction of per capita economic measures.

25. The number of full-time, full-year workers in families increased by about 18 percent between 1983 and 1988, while the number of full-time, full-year workers who were single increased by more than 30 percent.

26. This assumes an annually compounded real interest rate averaging 3 percent over those 35 years. This rate is somewhat higher than the real interest rates of the 1950s and 1960s, about equal to the rates of the late 1970s, and significantly lower than today's rates.

27. See, for example, Kuttner (1987), Glastris (1990), and Farnham (1990).

28. This is really an extension of consumption and savings analyses because the presence of a bequest motive implies a tendency to save rather than spend one's income and wealth.

29. Danziger et al. (1982) and Menchik and Martin (1983).

30. Hurd (1987), p. 306.

31. The experience of the 1929–1938 cohort, the "parents" of the baby boomers, is also projected forward for ten years using the same lower bound assumptions. This allows us to compare the net wealth of each cohort on the table in the years just prior to retirement. The basis for these figures is Greenwood and Wolff (1988). Their values for 1983 are somewhat higher than our own (shown in tables 5.7, 5.10 and 5.11), using the same Survey of Consumer Finances data, because they made various upward adjustments to match aggregate net wealth data. Values by education group were generated using proportional calculations from our 1983 tabulations.

Chapter Eight

POLICIES FOR THE NEXT GENERATION

In this book we have discussed trends and prospects for American families in income and wealth. We have shown that productivity and general economic growth slowed considerably during the period after 1973 and that this depressed the growth of earnings and family income relative to earlier decades. The earnings and income slowdown affected all workers but hurt young male workers the most. Furthermore, the less educated fared uniformly worse than the more educated. Between 1973 and 1986, the earnings of young men with four years of college, for example, just about kept pace with inflation, while the earnings of those with only four years of high school declined by 16 percent in inflation-adjusted terms.

WHERE FAMILIES STAND

The general decline in earnings has in part led to a situation in which more and more families must have multiple earners in order to enhance their standard of living. Coupled with an increase in the proportion of children being raised in single-parent families, earnings growth stagnation is increasing inequality across the general family income distribution. Young families *without* two earners appear to be falling further behind in their efforts to achieve upward mobility. Since a higher proportion of black families are single-parent families, and thus have at most one earner, young black families have experienced a decline in their economic status relative to young white families. And white *and* black young families have fared worse than older families.

The growth in net wealth also slowed dramatically in the 1970s, but this decline began prior to 1973. Again, this slowdown affected

young families the most because older families had already accumulated a substantial amount of net wealth when the slowdown
began. As was the case with income growth, those families headed
by persons with at least some college appear to have done considerably better than those headed by persons with less education. The
less educated are less likely to own a home, the principal component
of family net wealth and, even if they do, they are less likely to have
other forms of net wealth that would help protect them from declines
in the housing market.

These trends create a very uncertain future for the younger cohorts
of American families. The recent performance of the U.S. economy,
although improved significantly from the 1970s, has not matched
the growth of the 1950s and 1960s. Most economists, including the
major macroeconomic forecasting firms, believe that the near future
will be very much more like the recent rather than the distant past.
This means steady but slow economic growth and thus no acceleration in real earnings and income growth that would compensate
workers for the unspectacular growth prior to 1984.

Furthermore, demographic trends appear likely to undermine the
growth in general housing demand. This will be a two-edged sword
for American families. On the one hand, the absence of the demographic pressures that created so many new households in the 1970s
may increase housing affordability for many young persons. This
will be particularly true if real income growth is stronger than the
growth in home values. On the other hand, as home values stabilize,
home equity growth will slow. Thus, although owning a home will
continue to be the cornerstone of net wealth for most families, broad
increases in home equity can no longer be relied upon to drive up
the real net wealth of many American families.

The trends in future net wealth growth are therefore likely to favor
those who already have substantial and diversified net wealth holdings. Continuation of today's high real interest rates, for example,
will favor those who have cash to lend, principally members of older
generations.

These signs all point to a more difficult time for younger generations than for older ones. Relative to their parents and older siblings,
today's young families will experience lower income and wealth
growth. Part of this is due to the good fortune of those older generations, whose principal years in the labor force (the 1950s and
1960s) were marked by U.S. economic growth that was unprece-
dented and may never be duplicated.

The Importance of Education

The more educated young are less likely than their less educated peers to perceive that they have fallen behind the performance of previous generations. Relatively stronger wage growth, a greater ability to enter the housing market, and substantially higher and more diversified net wealth holdings will insulate them in part from the lackluster U.S. economic performance. It is the less educated young who will see the greatest declines in their economic status as a result of these trends, which will make them less likely to obtain and keep a job that provides a "middle class" standard of living. Partially as a result of this and partially as a result of high real interest rates, in the 1990s the less educated will be even less likely to own a home than they are today. These financial pressures may be sufficient to break up existing families or prevent the formation of new ones, thus eliminating the possibility that lesser educated families could maintain their living standards by having two earners.

Getting an education by itself, of course, does not guarantee financial success. There must, after all, be an increase in demand for educated labor to match the increase in supply. But it seems that with the growing complexity of tasks in manufacturing and other industries, education may have become a more important element in determining the career and earnings paths of individuals in the 1980s than it was in the 1950s and 1960s when all wages were growing rapidly.

GOVERNMENT POLICIES: PROBLEMS AND RECOMMENDATIONS

What can government policies do to alter these prospects? To begin to answer this question, it is useful to review the context in which future policy will operate by reconsidering the history of the post-World War II United States described in chapters 2 and 4. Implicit in that history was the distinction between equality and mobility. Throughout the post-war period, the U.S. economy never produced earnings distributions that were very equal. In 1969, the year of greatest family income equality, the richest one-fifth of families still received about $7.40 of income for every $1.00 of income received by the poorest one-fifth.

Although the pie was unevenly distributed, it was growing fast. The *relative* gaps between rich and poor remained, but most families were getting richer in absolute terms: they saw significant progress in their own lives, progress vis-à-vis their parents, and progress with respect to other fixed benchmarks. In this way, the economy's rapid growth produced a mass upward mobility that permitted issues of equality such as substantial income redistribution to be sidestepped.

Since 1973 the slowdown of economic growth has similarly put the brakes on economic mobility, but with different effects on different groups. In particular, the reader may ask: "Suppose that today's middle-class child does not live any better than his or her parents did. What's so bad about that?" If that were the end of the story, it wouldn't be a bad story at all.

But as we have seen in these chapters, a reduction in mobility is not evenly distributed across individuals. If today's college-educated workers will earn a little more than their college-educated parents did, today's high-school-educated workers may well earn less. And slow growth also helps to create differentially bad conditions at the bottom of the income distribution, where there remains a significant proportion of children with poor prospects of even finishing high school.[1]

A national administration may well recognize the structure of this problem: when economic growth is slow a population is tempted to keep its consumption growing by reducing savings and investment, including investment in human resources like low-income children. But should the administration want to act, the differential impact of slow growth described above raises a serious obstacle. If middle and upper income groups—the groups who are most politically active—are experiencing relatively little current pain, they will not be clamoring for policy changes to deal with the situation.

The policy context contains a second related problem, the absence of a big shock to the system. The U.S. political system changes direction best in reaction to a major event that can galvanize public opinion: a sudden sharp recession, the launching of Sputnik, a major airline disaster. The growth slowdown we have described in these chapters has been and may continue to be free of any such galvanizing event. To the contrary, each day looks very much like the last so that the loss of large-scale upward mobility proceeds without a constituency for changed policies.

These two facts, that economic pain rises from the bottom up and that the pain grows without dramatic shocks mean that any president willing to confront these issues would have to display remarkable leadership. If an administration were willing to attempt such leadership, it would begin to work in three areas:

□ Increasing the individual skills of the current labor force;
□ Increasing national savings and investment by both eliminating the federal deficit and encouraging young families to save a higher proportion of their disposable income;
□ Encouraging students to complete high school and if possible to obtain more advanced educational and technical credentials in order to have marketable skills when they enter the labor force.

Increasing Current Labor Force Skills

Since the middle of 1987, the unemployment rate in the U.S. has been at or near the level that economists formerly considered to be full employment. Even for the two years prior to that, the unemployment rate had been steadily and dramatically falling, from 7.0 percent in mid-1985 to 6.0 percent in mid-1987. Furthermore, labor productivity has been rising, albeit at a rate considerably below U.S. post-World War II standards.

Traditional economic thought predicts that rising productivity combined with a tightening labor market should lead to rising real earnings for all workers. Yet, as we have shown, younger workers with less education have not been able to maintain their wage growth at a level to match even today's relatively low inflation levels.

The reasons for this are not entirely understood. Some earnings stagnation is almost certainly due to localized cyclical labor surpluses such as those seen today in oil-producing sections of the country and in some depressed urban areas. Some may be due to poor work habits by young workers who experienced long labor force disruptions during periods of high unemployment in the early 1980s, just as they started their working careers.

However, some of the wage stagnation problem is caused by poor matches between the skills required by new technologies (such as computerized production lines) across industries and the skills of the labor force. A 1989 report by the Department of Labor's Commission on Workforce Quality and Labor Market Efficiency identified this as the key problem in today's labor market.[2] These mismatches should be correctable and some firms are taking the initiative to train workers in the required skills or to adapt production techniques so that workers are better able to utilize them.

It is not clear that government either should or needs to have a direct role in providing financial or tax incentives for firms to train their own workforces. Larger and richer firms are likely voluntarily to initiate in-house training programs to compensate for tight labor markets and lower skilled entry-level workers. Smaller firms are more likely to try to hire workers trained by the larger firms. In either case, such activities will lead to an improvement in the skills match in those labor markets where labor is in short supply.

The government's role may be one of identifying the skills required by industries in order to allow programs to be developed to train workers in those skills. Additionally, to the extent that mismatches result from regional shifts in labor supply and demand, the government may be able to report on where labor shortages are. Thus, the federal government's policies may be to exhort industry to compensate for skill mismatches and to facilitate the exchange of technologies to retrain workers and improve productive efficiency.

Increasing Family Savings

As we have shown in chapter 7, young families today, particularly those who have only recently entered the housing market, will not be able to rely on rising home equity to build a substantial amount of net wealth by the time they retire.[3] And only a small number will be able to take advantage of inherited wealth as a source of financial security. For most families then, the only way to increase net wealth as they age is to decrease their current consumption and increase their personal savings.

The federal government has in recent years moved to decrease personal income tax rates in order to increase disposable income. Ideally, this should have led to increases in personal savings. But, as tables 7.4 and 7.7 show, although young families appear to have modestly increased the percentage of income they saved between 1981 and 1986, overall per worker savings declined between 1983 and 1988. At the same time, per worker consumption increased significantly. Thus, it appears that nonspecific tax reductions may be more likely to lead to increased consumption rather than increased savings.

What else can be done? One possibility is for both the government and the private sector to embark upon an information campaign to convince today's workers that they cannot expect the same kind of good fortune in their net wealth growth that helped their parents' generation achieve such high levels of real wealth.

Beyond such frank talk, the federal government may need to publish minimum guidelines on what people *ought* to save: a simple schedule that relates annual savings to family income and age. In an uncertain world, disinterested rules of thumb can be powerful guides. The cover story in the July 31, 1989 issue of *Fortune* magazine ("Will You Be Able to Retire?") was an article along these lines. The author concluded that many of today's workers would have to save between 10 and 20 percent of their income to retire on an income equivalent to 70 percent of their final earnings even if they were covered by a company pension plan. Young self-employed workers might have to save 35 percent of their current disposable income to guarantee such a replacement income.[4]

The government could also provide incentives for families to save more and consume less. President Bush made a modest start toward this in 1990 with his Family Savings Plan proposal, which would allow families to defer taxes on interest in special accounts. Among other current policy proposals are ones to disregard a certain portion of interest and dividends from taxable income, restore the tax deductibility of Individual Retirement Account contributions to all workers, and create special purpose IRAs for young families to buy their first homes or for parents to finance their children's higher education. A politically less palatable suggestion, promoted by many economists, is to create a national sales tax such as a Value Added Tax, which would presumably depress consumption and make savings more attractive.

These policy proposals are subject to uncertain behavioral outcomes. As noted earlier, tax policies sometimes do not have the intended impacts on behavior. Barnes and Jefferson (1984), for example, reported that participation in IRAs tended to be much higher among home owners and the college educated during the late 1970s and early 1980s. Based on our analysis, however, these are precisely the families who least need to save for their retirement. Increased saving is most likely to benefit the non-college educated and non-home owners in spite of the fact that, because of consumption pressures, it may prove more difficult for these groups to save substantial amounts of income. Tax plans that allow deductions for contributions to special home down payment and educational accounts are also likely to experience disproportionate participation by the more fortunate young. And it is generally believed that tax incentives for special purpose savings simply displace savings that would have occurred in any event. Furthermore, a national consumption tax such as a value added tax would generally be income regressive since lower income families spend a higher proportion of their income.

These complexities do not necessarily eliminate these tax options as effective tools in stimulating increased savings among the lesser educated. But they do show that the proposals need to be framed carefully if they are to be effective among the individuals and families who are most likely to benefit from increased savings. A possible modification of the special purpose tax deduction proposals, for example, may involve phasing out the deduction after certain income limits are exceeded. Additionally, since participation in these tax plans will be voluntary, it may be better to focus on savings for purposes that have shorter run impacts on the young. Home down payment accounts where tax liabilities are deferred until capital gains are realized, for example, may be more attractive to young, less educated family heads than retirement accounts where the major benefits of targeted savings are in the distant future.

The precise formulation of tax proposals in this area is best left to the policymakers in the U.S. Treasury Department and the tax writing committees on Capitol Hill. But because tax policies affect all workers and are reasonably well understood by the general populace, they seem to offer the best vehicle for changing the savings behavior of today's young families.

Finally, we should recognize that savings serves two roles in the story we have told. At an individual level, it provides the basis for a family's economic security. At a national level, it can provide the basis for increased capital accumulation, increased higher investment productivity, and higher living standards. In the best of times, higher savings rates and a resulting lower cost of capital are only one element in solving the productivity problem. But at the current time, even this element is substantially weakened because of the government budget deficit. In the period from 1984 through 1987, for example, individuals saved a total of $515 billion. During that same period, the federal budget deficit totaled $768 billion. National savings as a whole remained positive because businesses saved about three times as much as individuals. But these numbers suggest that the strongest lever the government has to increase funds available for investment is to cut back the federal deficit.

Educating the Young Prior to Entering the Labor Force

Public education became a popular political issue in the late 1980s. Much of this debate has centered around volatile issues at the elementary and secondary level such as the intelligence and commitment of today's children, the quality and pay of teachers, and the school and community environments in which the education occurs. Our income figures imply that although it is preferable for today's young adults (18 and older) to complete a secondary school education rather than drop out of elementary or high school, doing so does not guarantee that an individual will obtain a good middle-class job. However, getting an advanced degree appears to be an important factor in securing a job with earnings gains that will exceed the rate of inflation.

It is clear from this and other research that the financial returns to completing a college education are now quite considerable.[5] In 1987 the earnings of young men and women who had not completed high school were less than half the earnings of young men and women who had completed at least some college. For those who have the abilities and initiative, a college education seems the surest way to compete well in the labor market. The same will be true for the children of today's young parents.

The first step toward getting an advanced degree is completing high school. Figures from the Census Bureau show that for the vast majority of white children, the probability of completing high school is increasing. But while the probability of completing high school is also increasing for most black children, it is declining for some. If this becomes a significant trend, it must be reversed, or many of today's black children will face little hope of competing well in tomorrow's labor market. Similarly, our figures imply that more high school graduates should be encouraged to go on to higher education.

It is not yet known why the returns to education have increased so much since 1973. Among the possible explanations are that a college education provides technical training (i.e., in mathematics, business, or science) essential in today's labor markets, that attending college allows students to develop more mature attitudes toward work, and that the additional years of schooling help individuals decide on more satisfying and appropriate career paths. Because neither these processes nor the factors that affect the decisions of individual students to stop or continue their educations are well understood, the development of public policy to encourage more education is necessarily ad hoc.

The Department of Labor's Commission on Workforce Quality and Labor Market Efficiency, for example, has made more than three dozen recommendations including timetables and strategies for reducing dropout rates, increasing attendance rates, improving test scores, and getting parents and businesses more involved in elementary and secondary education. In 1988 the William T. Grant

Foundation's Commission on Youth and America's Future recommended that the federal government invest billions of dollars more in development programs such as Head Start and the Job Corps.[6] Other ideas at the higher education level have included expansions of government tuition assistance programs, strengthening of two-year and four-year public institutions of higher learning, and changes in college curricula to emphasize more marketable skills.

Like other public policies, many of these strategies are untested. It is impossible to predict at this point how effective any public policies can be at attracting urban black youth away from lucrative underground jobs, especially those related to the distribution of drugs, and into the legitimate labor market. But it may be that a broad effort to increase public awareness of the increasing financial returns to education will be at least partially successful in bringing the future skills of the labor force more into line with the needs of industry than they are today.

CONCLUSION

In the first chapter of this book we discussed the collective nature of the future: how future living standards depend on the aggregate condition of the future labor force and the future capital stock which, in turn, depend on hundreds and thousands of individual decisions. This "public good" aspect of today's economic problems seems to suggest a counsel of despair. If a family's future depends upon so many decisions that it cannot control, it may be tempted to ignore the future altogether.

To react this way is to make a big mistake. While a family cannot guarantee that its children will experience dramatic income gains (like those in the 1950s and 1960s), it can still ensure that its children do as well as possible in the context of the times by getting them a good education. Similarly, a family cannot guarantee by its savings that it will retire in a buoyant economy. But in any economy families who have accumulated assets will be better off than those who have not.

The same is true for us as a nation. The better educated our labor force and the higher our savings, the better off we shall be. The future of the economy, therefore, depends on the proportion of families who plan well for their future, and on the help society offers to those families and children who want to make provision for the future but do not have the resources. Political leadership is required to show us all that in terms of the economic future, we all have at least one foot in the same boat, and that our individual economic futures depend on both our behavior as individuals and our behavior as a nation.

Notes

1. The argument we are sketching here is not "trickle down" economics. The trickle down theory holds that rapid economic growth is *caused* by giving more money to the well-off (who in turn invest it, etc.). We are saying here that if, for any reason, a slowdown in the overall rate of economic growth occurs, persons with higher educations, etc., are likely to remain in comfortable situations long after persons further down in the income distribution have seen serious economic dislocations.

2. U.S. Department of Labor (1989). There is an alternative view, which is that the "Workforce 2000" report, as the Labor Department study is known, overstates the growth in high-skilled occupations and that the real problem is rooted in shifts in business investment from labor to capital. See Teixeira and Mishel (1990).

3. There will, of course, be exceptions to this because of variations in local housing markets. See chapter 7 for a full discussion.

4. Kirkpatrick (1989).

5. See, for example, Levy and Michel (1988) and Blackburn, Bloom, and Freeman (1990).

6. See the William T. Grant Foundation (1988).

ACCOUNTING FOR SOCIAL SECURITY AND PENSIONS IN NET WEALTH

As we discuss in the main body of this book, the accumulation of wealth can come from sources such as inheritances, the growth in the value of assets, or savings from income.[1] For the average family, the major component of wealth is the equity it has in its principal residence. Other assets such as savings accounts, stocks and bonds, other real property, interest in a business, art objects, and other valuable material holdings are also included in the conventionally accepted profile of the wealth status of a household.

In spite of this consensus in the popular concept of wealth, there is much disagreement among economic analysts over what the true components of wealth are and how to measure them. While there are several potential components that are the subject of dispute, a particularly troublesome conceptual issue is whether and how to account for future social security benefits or any deferred benefits under a defined benefit pension plan. The potential present dollar value of future flows from these sources is in the hundreds of billions of dollars, so this issue is not trivial. Some studies have excluded social security benefits from wealth computations, others have included them as the present value of the expected stream of benefits to which an individual would be entitled.[2]

On the one hand, of course, social security benefits do represent a form of wealth in that, at least until now, benefits have been guaranteed upon retirement. Some analysts have argued that this guarantee alters the inclination of individuals to save for their own retirement and that this lower savings propensity is evidence that people implicitly treat social security benefits as net wealth.[3]

On the other hand, the payment of social security benefits is subject to uncertain future political decisions and the benefits themselves represent at best a restricted asset in that they cannot be bequeathed, borrowed against, or transferred. Other analysts have thus argued that implicit social security guarantees do not substantially substitute for private savings and that at least some analyses which ostensibly show that there are large displacement effects are the result of misspecifications.[4]

The tentative nature of the future payment of benefits has been brought home in recent years, first, by the Social Security Amendments of 1983 which taxed 50 percent of benefits for individuals and couples above certain annual income thresholds[5] and, second, by an increasing number of proposals to tax as much as 85 percent of benefits in the future.[6] Furthermore, the 1983 (current) law does not adjust the income thresholds for inflation. This means that in the future, as incomes rise, more and more of the retired will have their benefits subject to taxation.[7]

Similar arguments have been waged over the treatment of private pensions in defined benefit plans. These plans, where funding is provided by the employer and benefits paid under a formula linked to wages and salaries or tenure or both, apply to over 70 percent of all private pension participants.[8] But, similar to the case of social security, future benefits in such pension plans are a function of the uncertain financial viability of company or union pension funds.[9]

While the disagreement over whether social security and defined benefit pension plans displace savings may seem somewhat tangential to the issue of measuring net wealth, it is not. If individuals accept the promise of future benefits from the Social Security Administration and their employers as certain, that is they perceive these promises to be the equivalent of personal savings, then it might seem reasonable to include them in any wealth analyses.

We believe the perception/behavior argument is a *necessary* condition to including these public and private retirement payments in wealth but is not a *sufficient* argument. There are several other conditions which would seem to be required to categorize these payments as the equivalent of, say, a savings account. First, payment must be near certain. The perception of certainty by potential recipients is not adequate in the analysis of economic well-being though it may be for the analysis of savings behavior. For social security, full payment of benefits is not certain since that would require future retirement income to be below the taxation thresholds discussed above. For defined benefit pensions, similar uncertainty exists because of the essentially unfunded pension liabilities of many corporations.

Second, access to the funds must be more or less unrestricted. Neither social security nor many defined benefit pension plans are capable of being cashed in by the recipient, even though spousal payments may continue after the death of the principal pension holder.

Finally, neither social security nor defined benefit pensions are transferable to heirs. For these latter reasons, some analysts have argued that if one includes social security and defined benefit pensions in net wealth, the current cash surrender value rather than present value of future income flows should be the preferred method of measuring their worth. For private pensions, Edward Wolff estimates the cash surrender value at five percent of total current reserves. For social security, the cash surrender value for current workers would be zero.[10]

Because of these arguments, the conceptual basis for including social security and private pension payments in family net wealth studies seems unpersuasive. In essence, these pension programs are more like income entitlements than either liquid or illiquid assets and should be treated in a similar manner. In the case of poor or disabled persons, for example, we would not consider including the present value of future welfare payments (e.g., benefits from the Aid to Families with Dependent Children or Supplemental Security Income programs) in net wealth even though we might argue that these payments cause families with such payments to alter their economic behavior.

These conceptual arguments about the inclusion of social security and pension benefits in net wealth are compounded by several related technical factors. Measurement of the exact present value of social security or defined pension benefits is virtually impossible at the individual level, unless the individual is on the verge of retirement. Estimating the value of social security to a 35-year-old, for example, requires some forecast of his or her future income and particularly income in the ten years or so prior to retirement. The forecast of this future income is dependent upon both labor demand and labor supply decisions, including the decision of an individual to retire at a particular age. A further measurement problem related to private pensions is that future contributions by companies are essentially unknown and that benefit formulae are very difficult to enumerate (owing mostly to the large number of company and union pension plans). The result is that analysts generally only know what the aggregate national balance of funds are today and that only through the flawed national income and product accounts.[11]

In practice then, most methods of accounting for social security and private pension wealth rely on adding them to aggregate measures of wealth. Distributing these balances across families is simply too difficult a task. This means that we cannot account for the differential present value of these payments by such factors as income or age.

The inability to disaggregate by age is particular important for the analysis in this volume. Future retirees, that is today's younger workers, are likely to receive lower net social security benefits than today's elderly for two reasons. First, current taxation policies with respect to social security benefits will result in a higher proportion of baby boomers having their benefits subject to taxation than the proportion of current retirees. Second, because of a gradual increase in the full retirement age, most baby boomers will be able to receive "full" benefits only at age 67 rather than 65 as is currently true. For almost all of the analysis contained in this volume, the available information and technologies are therefore inadequate even if one accepts the conceptual arguments in favor of including social security and pensions in family wealth.

Do we have any indication of how much difference such an inclusion would make if we were able to measure the value of social security and private pensions properly? Wolff (1989) reports that the inclusion of the present value of private pensions would add about 13 percent to *aggregate* real net wealth in 1983.[12] But the addition of the present value of social security benefits would add another 50 percent. This is clearly significant.

Furthermore, while the pre-1969 growth rates in *per household* net wealth are fairly stable across these wealth definitions, the inclusion of both private pensions and social security actually alters the sign of average annual changes in the period from 1969 to 1983. Excluding private pensions and social security, real net wealth per household in that period *declined* by an average of .17 percent per year. Including the present value of these two items, real net wealth per household, *grew* by an average of .35 percent per year.

Thus, we concede that inclusion of such benefits in net wealth might alter some of the trends described in this volume. In general, we feel these inclusions would show that current retirees and retirees of the near future (the older generations) would be even better off relative to younger individuals than some of our results imply, even though, in absolute terms, all families would be better off.

Notes

1. Or from the corollary of savings, debt reduction.
2. See, for example, Wolff and Marley (1989) or Wolff (1989) who have done it both ways.

3. See, for example, Feldstein (1983). In this article, Feldstein estimates that social security wealth reduces private savings dollar for dollar. This implies that individuals consider future social security benefits the equivalent of present personal savings. To his credit, Feldstein also reviews the arguments against including social security in wealth calculations.

4. See Leimer and Lesnoy (1982) who reanalyzed the data in Feldstein (1974).

5. The threshold for single persons is $25,000 and for couples is $32,000.

6. See, for example, Ford Foundation (1989), Chapter 6.

7. Sheila Zedlewski of The Urban Institute, using the DYNASIM model, has estimated that by the year 2030, more than 80 percent of the elderly will be paying federal income taxes. See Michel, Storey and Zedlewski (1983), Chapter 4.

8. See Kotlikoff and Smith (1983).

9. In general, defined-*contribution* plans where both the employee and employer contribute to an account which accumulates and compounds over the period of employment *and* belongs to the employee are included as personal wealth.

10. See Wolff (1989), Section I for a discussion of this issue.

11. For a discussion of the NIPA deficiencies, see Hendershott and Peek (1985).

12. The inclusion of private pensions at cash surrender value adds less than one percent to aggregate net wealth.

REFERENCES

Apgar, William C. Jr., H. James Brown, George Masnick, and John Pitkin. 1985. *The Housing Outlook: 1980–1990*. New York: Praeger Publishers.

Astin, A. W. et al. 1989. "The American Freshman: National Norms for Fall 1989." Los Angeles, California: Cooperative Institutional Research Program of the American Council on Education and the University of California at Los Angeles.

Avery, Robert B. and Gregory Elliehausen. 1986. "Financial Characteristics of High Income Families." *Federal Reserve Bulletin* 72, no. 3 (March): 163–177.

Avery, Robert B., Gregory E. Elliehausen, and Glenn B. Canner. 1984a. "Survey of Consumer Finances, 1983." *Federal Reserve Bulletin* 70, no. 9 (September): 679–692.

————. 1984b. "Survey of Consumer Finances, 1983: A Second Report." *Federal Reserve Bulletin* 70, no. 12 (December): 857–868.

Avery, Robert B. and Arthur B. Kennickell. 1988. "1986 Survey of Consumer Finances: Technical Manual and Codebook." Washington, D.C.: Board of Governors of the Federal Reserve System, October 24, 1988.

Baily, Martin Neil and Alok K. Chakrabarti. 1988. *Innovation and the Productivity Crisis*. Washington, D.C.: The Brookings Institution.

Baily, Martin Neil and Robert J. Gordon. 1988. "The Productivity Slowdown, Measurement Issues, and the Explosion of Computer Power." *Brookings Papers on Economic Activity*, no. 2: 347–421.

Bailey, Thomas. 1988. "Education and the Transformation of Markets and Technology in the Textile Industry." Technical Paper No. 2. New York: Columbia University Teachers' College National Center on Education and Employment, April.

Bane, Mary Jo and David T. Ellwood. 1986. "Slipping In and Out of Poverty: The Dynamics of Spells." *Journal of Human Resources* 21, no. 1 (Winter): 1–23.

Barnes, Roberta O. and Linda Giannarelli Jefferson. 1984. "Individual Savings for Retirement: New Evidence on IRA Participation." Working Paper No. 3192-01. Washington, D.C.: The Urban Institute.

Bassi, Lauri J. 1987. "Family Structure and Poverty among Women and Children: What Accounts for the Change." Mimeo. Washington, D.C.: Georgetown University, June.

Bianchi, Suzanne M. and Daphne Spain. 1986. *American Women In Transition*. New York: The Russell Sage Foundation.

Bishop, John H. 1989. "Is the Test Score Decline Responsible for the Productivity Growth Decline?" *American Economic Review* 79, no. 1 (March): 178–197.

Blackburn, McKinley, David Bloom, and Richard B. Freeman. 1990. "The Declining Economic Position of Less Skilled American Men." In G. Burtless, ed., *A Future of Lousy Jobs? The Changing Structure of U.S. Wages*. Washington, D.C.: The Brookings Institution.

Blanchard, Olivier J. and Lawrence H. Summers. 1986. "Hysteresis and the European Unemployment Problem." In *National Bureau of Economic Research Macroeconomics Annual*. Cambridge, MA: MIT Press 15–78.

Blick, P. and S. L. Lin. 1986. "More Young Adults are Living with their Parents: Who are They?" *Journal of Marriage and Family*, no. 48: 107–112.

Bluestone, Barry, and Bennett Harrison. 1986. "The Great American Job Machine: The Proliferation of Low-Wage Employment in the U.S. Economy." Study prepared for the Joint Economic Committee of the U.S. Congress. Washington, D.C., December.

Boskin, Michael J. and Lawrence J. Lau. 1988. "An Analysis of Postwar U.S. Consumption and Saving." Research Paper. Palo Alto, CA: Stanford University Center for Economic Policy Research.

Bosworth, Barry P. 1988. "Recent Trends in Private Saving." Paper presented at the annual meetings of the American Economic Association, New York, December 19.

Brookes, Warren T. 1987. "Low-Pay Jobs: The Big Lie." *The Wall Street Journal* (op-ed), March 25.

Butz, William P. and Michel P. Ward. 1979. "The Emergence of Counter-Cyclical U.S. Fertility." *American Economic Review* 69, no. 3 (June): 318–328.

Coder, John, Lee Rainwater, and Timothy Smeeding. 1988. "Inequality among Children and Elderly in Ten Modern Nations: The U.S. in an International Context." Paper prepared at the American Economic Association Meetings, New York, December.

Children's Defense Fund. 1988. *A Call for Action to Make Our Nation Safe For Children: A Briefing Book on the Status of American Children in 1988*. Washington, D.C.

Data Resources, Inc. 1989. *U.S. Cost Information Service Long-Term Review*. 15, no. 1 (January). Lexington, MA: Data Resources, Inc.

Danziger, Sheldon, Jacques van der Gaag, Eugene Smolensky, and Michael Taussig. 1982. "The Life-Cycle Hypothesis and the Consumption

Behavior of the Elderly." *Journal of Post-Keynesian Economics* 5, no. 2 (Winter): 208–227.

Dennison, Edward F. 1985. *Trends in American Economic Growth, 1929–82.* Washington, D.C.: The Brookings Institution.

Downs, Anthony. 1989. "High Home Prices: A Worldwide Problem." Bond Market Research Report, Real Estate. New York: Salomon Brothers, March.

Easterlin, Richard. 1980. *Birth and Fortune.* New York: Basic Books.

Elster, Susan and Mark S. Kamlet. 1987. "Income Aspirations and Married Women's Labor Force Participation." Mimeo. Pittsburgh, PA: Carnegie Mellon University, September 21.

Farnham, Alan. 1990. "The Windfall Awaiting the New Inheritors." *Fortune.* May 7, 72–78.

Feldstein, Martin. 1983. "Social Security Benefits and the Accumulation of Pre-Retirement Wealth." In F. Modigliani and R. Hemming, eds., *The Determinants of National Savings and Wealth.* New York: St. Martin's Press, 3–33.

————. 1974. "Social Security, Induced Retirement and Aggregate Capital Accumulation." *Journal of Political Economy* 82 (October): 905–926.

Freeman, Richard B. 1976. *The Overeducated American.* New York: Academic Press.

Ford Foundation Project on Social Welfare and the American Future. 1989. "The Common Good: Social Welfare and the American Future." New York: The Ford Foundation.

Fuchs, Victor R. 1968. *The Service Economy.* New York: National Bureau of Economic Research and Columbia University Press.

————. 1988. *Women's Quest for Economic Equality.* Cambridge, MA: Harvard University Press.

Gans, Herbert. 1967. *The Levittowners.* New York: Pantheon Books.

Glastris, Paul. 1990. "The New Way to Get Rich." *U.S. News and World Report,* May 7, 27–36.

Gottschalk, Peter, Sheldon Danziger, and Eugene Smolensky. 1988. "Recent Developments in the Upper Tail of the Income Distribution." Paper prepared for the Annual Meetings of the American Economic Association, New York, December.

Greenwood, Daphne T. 1987. "Age, Income and Household Size: Their Relation to Wealth Distribution in the United States." In E. N. Wolff, ed., *International Comparisons of the Distribution of Household Wealth.* Oxford, England: Clarendon Press.

Greenwood, Daphne T. and Edward N. Wolff. 1989. "Changes in Wealth: Life-Cycle, Period and Cohort Effects in the United States, 1962–83." Paper presented at the Third Annual Conference of the European Society for Population Economics. Domaine de Fremigny, France, June 8–11.

_____. 1988. "Relative Wealth Holdings of Children and the Elderly in the United States, 1962–83." In J. L. Palmer, T. Smeeding, and B. B. Torrey, eds., *The Vulnerable*. Washington, D.C.: Urban Institute Press, 123–148.

Helliwell, John F. 1990. "The Fiscal and External Deficits: Siblings But Not Twins." In Rudolph G. Penner, ed., *The Great Fiscal Experiment*. Washington, D.C.: Urban Institute Press.

Hendershott, Patric H. 1985. "An Overview." In P. H. Hendershott, ed., *The Level and Composition of Household Saving*. Cambridge, MA: Ballinger Publishing Company, 3–14.

Hendershott, Patric H. and Joe Peek. 1985. "Household Saving: An Econometric Investigation." In P. H. Hendershott, ed., *The Level and Composition of Household Saving*. Cambridge, MA: Ballinger Publishing Company, 63–100.

Herrnstein, R. J. 1989. "IQ and Falling Birth Rates." *The Atlantic Monthly* (May): 72–79.

Horvath, Francis W. 1987. "The Pulse of Economic Change: Displaced Workers 1981–85." *Monthly Labor Review* 10, no. 7 (July): 3–12.

Hurd, Michael D. 1987. "Savings of the Elderly and Desired Bequests." *American Economic Review* 77, no. 3 (June): 298–312.

Johnston, William and Arnold Packer. 1987. *Workforce 2000 Report*. Washington, D.C.: The Hudson Institute and the U.S. Department of Labor.

Joint Center for Housing Studies of Massachusetts Institute of Technology and Harvard University. 1985. "Home Ownership and Housing Affordability in the United States: 1963–85." Cambridge, MA: Joint Center for Housing Studies.

_____. 1989. "The State of the Nation's Housing, 1989." Cambridge, MA: Joint Center for Housing Studies.

Katona, George, Charles A. Lininger, and Richard F. Kosobud. 1963. *1962 Survey of Consumer Finances*. Monograph no. 32. Ann Arbor, MI: University of Michigan Survey Research Center.

Katz, Lawrence F. and Lawrence H. Summers. 1988. "Can Inter-Industry Wage Differentials Justify Strategic Trade Policy?" Mimeo. Cambridge, MA: National Bureau of Economic Research, April.

Kendrick, John. 1984. "The Implications of Growth Accounting Models." In Charles R. Hulten and Isabel V. Sawhill, eds., *The Legacy of Reaganomics: Prospects for Long Term Growth*. Washington, D.C.: Urban Institute Press, 19–44.

Kirkpatrick, David. 1989. "Will You Be Able to Retire?" *Fortune*. July 31: 56–66.

Kosters, Marvin H. and Murray N. Ross. 1988. "A Shrinking Middle Class?" *The Public Interest*, no. 90 (Winter): 3–27.

Kotlikoff, Laurence J. and Daniel E. Smith. 1983. *Pensions in the American Economy*. Chicago: University of Chicago Press.

Kotlikoff, Laurence J. and Lawrence Summers. 1981. "The Role of Intergenerational Transfers in Aggregate Capital Accumulation." *Journal of Political Economy* 89, no. 2 (August): 706–732.

Krein, Sheila Fitzgerald and Andrea H. Beller. 1989. "Educational Attainment of Children from Single-Parent Families: Differences by Exposure, Gender and Race." *Demography* 25, no. 2 (May): 221–234.

Kristol, Irving. 1980. "Comment" [on Alan Blinder's chapter]. In Martin Feldstein, ed., *The American Economy in Transition*. Cambridge, MA: National Bureau of Economic Research and University of Chicago Press.

Kuttner, Robert. 1983. "The Declining Middle." *The Atlantic Monthly*. July: 60–72.

————. 1987. "The Patrimony Society: What Happens When the First Generation of Mass Affluence Passes On?" *The New Republic*. May 11, 18–21.

Lansing, John B. and John Sonquist. 1969. "A Cohort Analysis of Changes in the Distribution of Wealth." In L. Soltow, ed., *Six Papers on the Size Distribution of Wealth and Income*. New York: National Bureau of Economic Research.

Lawrence, Robert Z. 1988. "The International Dimension." In Robert E. Litan, Robert Z. Lawrence, and Charles L. Schultze, eds., *American Living Standards: Threats and Challenges*. Washington, D.C.: The Brookings Institution, 23–65.

————. 1982. *Can America Compete?* Washington, D.C., The Brookings Institution.

Lawrence, Robert Z. and Charles L. Schultze, eds. 1987. *Barriers to European Growth: A Transatlantic View*. Washington, D.C., The Brookings Institution.

Leimer, Dean R. and Selig D. Lesnoy. 1982. "Social Security and Private Saving: New Time Series Evidence." *Journal of Political Economy* 90, no. 3 (June): 606–621.

Leonard, Paul A., Cushing N. Dolbeare, and Edward B. Lazere. 1989. "A Place to Call Home: The Crisis in Housing for the Poor." Washington, D.C.: Center for Budget and Policy Priorities, April.

Levin, Henry M. and Russell W. Rumberger. 1987. "Educational Requirements for New Technologies: Visions, Possibilities and Current Realities." *Educational Policy* 57, no. 3 (Fall): 101–109.

Levy, Frank. 1979. "On Understanding Proposition 13." *The Public Interest*, no. 56 (Summer): 66–89.

————. 1988a. *Dollars and Dreams: The Changing American Income Distribution*. New York, W.W. Norton.

————. 1988b. "Incomes, Families and Living Standards." In Robert E. Litan, Robert Z. Lawrence, and Charles L. Schultze, eds., *American Living Standards: Threats and Challenges*. Washington, D.C.: The Brookings Institution, 108–153.

Levy, Frank and Richard C. Michel. 1988. "Education and Income: Recent U.S. Trends." Report on the U.S. Congress Joint Economic Committee. Washington, D.C.: The Urban Institute.

_____. 1986. "An Economic Bust for the Baby Boom." *Challenge* 29, no. 1 (March/April): 33–39.

_____. 1987. "Understanding the Low Wage Jobs Debate." Mimeo. Washington, D.C.: The Urban Institute.

Levy, Frank and Richard J. Murnane. 1989. "Jobs, Demography, and the Mismatch Hypothesis." Working Paper. College Park, Maryland: University of Maryland School of Public Affairs.

Lillard, Lee, James P. Smith, and Finis Welch. 1986. "What Do We Really Know about Wages?" *Journal of Political Economy* 94, no. 3 (June): 489–506.

Litan, Robert E., Robert Z. Lawrence and Charles L. Schultze. 1988. *American Living Standards: Threats and Challenges.* Washington, D.C.: The Brookings Institution.

Maddison, Angus. 1987. "Growth and Slowdown in Advanced Capitalist Economies: Techniques of Quantitative Assessment." *Journal of Economic Literature* 25, no. 2 (June): 649–698.

Mankiw, H. Gregory and David N. Weil. 1988. "The Baby Boom, the Baby Bust and the Housing Market." Working Paper no. 2794. Cambridge, MA: National Bureau of Economic Research, December.

McClanahan, Sara S. 1985. "Family Structure and the Reproduction of Poverty." *American Journal of Sociology* 90, no. 4 (August): 873–901.

McClanahan, Sara S. and Gary Sandifur. 1988. "Comment" [on paper by Robert Mare]. In Marta Tienda and Gary Sandifur, eds., *Divided Opportunity.* New York: Plenum Press, 58–61.

Menchik, Paul L. and Martin David. 1983. "Income Distribution, Lifetime Savings, and Bequests." *American Economic Review* 73, no. 4 (September): 672–690.

Michel, Richard C., J. R. Storey, and S. R. Zedlewski. 1983. "Saving Social Security: The Short- and Long-Run Effects of the 1983 Amendments." Changing Domestic Priorities Project Discussion Paper. Washington, D.C.: The Urban Institute.

Minarik, Joseph J. 1985. *Making Tax Choices.* Washington, D.C.: The Urban Institute Press.

Modigliani, Franco. 1966. "The Life Cycle Hypothesis of Saving, the Demand for Wealth and the Supply of Capital." *Social Research* 33, no. 2 (Summer): 160–217.

Modigliani, Franco and Richard Brumberg. 1954. "Utility Analysis and the Consumption Function: An Interpretation of Cross-Section Data." In K. Kurihara, ed., *Post-Keynesian Economics.* New Brunswick, NJ: Rutgers University Press.

Moynihan, Daniel Patrick. 1987. "Epilogue." In *Family and Nation.* New York: Harcourt, Brace, Jovanovich.

Murphy, Kevin and Finis Welch. 1988. "Wage Differentials in the 1980's: The Role of International Trade." Paper presented at the Mont Pelerin Society General Meeting, September 9.

Norwood, Janet. 1987. "The Job Machine Has Not Broken Down." *The New York Times*. February 22, section F, 3.

Noyelle, Thierry. 1988. "Changing Occupations and Skill Demands in the Banking and Insurance Industries." Working Paper. New York: Columbia University Teachers' College Center on Education and Employment.

Piore, Michael J. and Charles F. Sabel. 1984. *The Second Industrial Divide*. New York: Basic Books.

Radner, Daniel B. and Denton R. Vaughan. 1984. "The Joint Distribution of Wealth and Income for Age Groups, 1979." Technical Paper no. 33. Washington, D.C.: U.S. Social Security Administration Office of Research, Statistics and International Policy.

Rosenthal, Neal H. 1985. "The Shrinking Middle Class: Myth or Reality?" *Monthly Labor Review* 108, no. 3 (March): 3–10.

Samuelson, Robert J. 1987. "The American Job Machine." *Newsweek*. February 23, 57.

Sawhill, Isabel V. 1988. "Overview." In Isabel V. Sawhill, ed., *Challenge to Leadership: Economic and Social Issues for the Next Decade*. Washington, D.C.: Urban Institute Press, 1–32.

Sawyer, Malcolm. 1976. "Income Distribution in OECD Countries." Paris, OECD Occasional Studies, July.

Schumpeter, Joseph. 1942. *Capitalism, Socialism and Democracy*. New York: Harper Press.

Smith, James P. and Michael P. Ward. 1984. *Women's Wages and Work in the Twentieth Century*. Santa Monica, CA: Rand Corporation.

Smith, James P. and Finis R. Welch. 1989. "Black Economic Progress After Myrdal." *Journal of Economic Literature* 27, no. 2 (June): 519–564.

Stern, David and Charles Benson. 1989. "The Economic Theory of On-the-Job Training." Paper prepared for the Conference on Market Failure in Training. LaFollette Institute of Public Affairs, University of Wisconsin/Madison, May 11–12.

Stone, Charles. 1988. "International Trade." In Isabel V. Sawhill, ed., *Challenge to Leadership: Economic and Social Problems for the Next Decade*. Washington, D.C.: Urban Institute Press, 101–145.

Sum, Andrew and Neal Fogg. 1987. "Trends in Real Earnings and Incomes of Young Males in the U.S.: 1967–1985." Working Paper. Boston: Center for Labor Market Studies, Northeastern University.

Thurow, Lester C. 1984. "The Disappearance of the Middle Class." *New York Times*. February 5, section 3, 2.

U.S. Bureau of the Census. 1987a. "Marital Status and Living Arrangements, March 1986." *Current Population Reports*, Series P-20, no. 418, Washington, D.C.: Government Printing Office.

————. 1987b. "Money Income of Households, Families and Persons in the United States, 1986." *Current Population Reports*, Series P-60, no. 159, Washington, D.C., Government Printing Office.

U.S. Congressional Budget Office. 1988. "Trends in Family Income: 1970–1986." Washington, D.C.: Government Printing Office.

————. 1987. "The Changing Distribution of Federal Taxes: 1975–1990." Washington, D.C.: Government Printing Office.

U.S. Council of Economic Advisers. 1990. *Economic Report of the President, 1990.* Washington, D.C.: Government Printing Office, February.

————. 1989. *Economic Report of the President, 1989.* Washington, D.C.: Government Printing Office, January.

————. 1988. *The Economic Report of the President, 1988.* Washington, D.C.: Government Printing Office, February.

————. 1985. *The Economic Report of the President, 1985.* Washington, D.C.: Government Printing Office, January.

U.S. Department of Commerce. 1988. *Statistical Abstract of the United States, 1988.* Washington, D.C.: Government Printing Office.

U.S. Department of Labor, Secretary's Commission on Workforce Quality and Labor Market Efficiency. 1989. "Investing in People: A Strategy to Address America's Workforce Crisis." Washington, D.C.: U.S. Department of Labor.

Vernon, Raymond. 1966. "International Investment and International Trade in the Product Cycle." *Quarterly Journal of Economics* 81, no. 2 (May): 190–207.

Weicher, John C. and Susan B. Wachter. 1986. "The Distribution of Wealth Among Families: Increasing Inequality?" Paper presented at the American Enterprise Institute Seminar on the Family and American Welfare Policy, Washington, D.C., November 10.

William T. Grant Foundation. 1988. *The Forgotten Half: Non-College Youth in America.* An Interim Report from Youth and America's Future Project. Washington, D.C.: William T. Grant Foundation.

Wilson, William J. 1988. *The Truly Disadvantaged.* Chicago: University of Chicago Press.

Wolff, Edward N. 1989. "Trends in Aggregate Household Wealth in the U.S., 1900–1983." *Review of Income and Wealth*, Series 35, no. 1 (March): 1–29.

Wolff, Edward N. and Marcia Marley. 1989. "Long-Term Trends in U.S. Wealth Inequality: Methodological Issues and Results." In R. Lipsey and H. Tice, eds., *The Measurement of Savings, Investment and Wealth.* Studies of Income and Wealth, vol. 52. Chicago: University of Chicago Press, 765–839.

ABOUT THE AUTHORS

Frank S. Levy is professor of Public Affairs at the University of Maryland's School of Public Affairs. Mr. Levy has written extensively on trends in living standards and income inequality. His book *Dollars and Dreams: The Changing American Income Distribution* (Norton, 1987) has become a widely cited reference on postwar income trends in the United States. Levy has been analyzing income and welfare issues for twenty years. Prior to joining the University of Maryland faculty in 1981, he was a Senior Research Associate at The Urban Institute and before that taught for ten years at the University of California at Berkeley. Levy completed his undergraduate work at M.I.T. and received his Ph.D. in economics from Yale University.

Richard C. Michel has been the director of the Income and Benefits Policy Center at The Urban Institute since 1983. He specializes in analyzing income and wage distributional trends using large household-level data bases from the Bureau of the Census. He is the editor and co-author of a recent book on large computer models to analyze household data. He is also the co-author, with Mr. Levy, of several published articles and papers on trends in the income distribution. As a senior economist in the Office of the Secretary of Health and Human Services Mr. Michel was responsible for developing and presenting distributional analyses of President Jimmy Carter's two major welfare reform proposals. Prior to that, he was an associate analyst specializing in legislative analysis of transfer programs with the Congressional Budget Office. He received his undergraduate degree from Syracuse University and completed his graduate work at the Wharton Graduate division of the University of Pennsylvania.